Student's Book

Stage 6

English in a quarter of the time!

The Callan ® Method was first developed and published
in 1960 by R.K. T. Callan.
This edition was published for the international market in 2012.

Copyright © R.K.T. Callan 2012

Student's Book – Stage 6
ISBN 978-1-908954-17-6

CALLAN and the CALLAN logo are registered trade marks
of Callan Works Limited, used under licence by Callan Publishing Limited

Printed in the EU

Published by

CALLAN PUBLISHING LTD.
Orchard House, 45-47 Mill Way, Grantchester, Cambridge CB3 9ND
in association with CALLAN METHOD ORGANISATION LTD.

www.callan.co.uk

- Para obtener la traducción de este prefacio en español, visitar
www.callan.co.uk/preface/es

- Per una traduzione di questa prefazione in Italiano, visitare il sito
www.callan.co.uk/preface/it

- Para obter uma tradução deste prefácio em português, visite
www.callan.co.uk/preface/pt

- Z polskim tłumaczeniem tego wstępu można zapoznać się na stronie
www.callan.co.uk/preface/pl

- Pour obtenir la traduction de cette préface en français, rendez-vous sur le site
www.callan.co.uk/preface/fr

- Bu önsözün Türkçe çevirisi için aşağıdaki web adresini ziyaret edin
www.callan.co.uk/preface/tr

- 本序言的中文翻译，请访问
www.callan.co.uk/preface/ch

- 前書きの日本語版の翻訳は次ページをご覧ください
www.callan.co.uk/preface/jp

- اللطالع على ترجمة هذه المقدمة باللغة العربية يرجى زيارة
www.callan.co.uk/preface/ar

Welcome to the Callan Method

Learning English with the Callan™ Method is fast and effective!

The Callan Method is a teaching method created specifically to improve your English in an intensive atmosphere. The teacher is constantly asking questions, so you are hearing and using the language as much as possible. When you speak in the lesson, the teacher corrects your grammar and pronunciation mistakes, and you learn a lot from this correction.

The Callan Method teaches English vocabulary and grammar in a carefully programmed way, with systematic revision and reinforcement. In the lesson, there is a lot of speaking and listening practice, but there is also reading and writing so that you revise and consolidate what you have learned.

With the Callan Method, the teacher speaks quickly so that you learn to understand English when it is spoken at natural speed. This also means that everyone is concentrating hard all the time.

English in a quarter of the time

The Callan Method can teach English in a quarter of the time taken by any other method on the market. Instead of the usual 350 hours necessary to get the average student to the level of the Cambridge Preliminary English Test (PET), the Callan Method can take as little as 80 hours, and only 160 hours for the Cambridge First Certificate in English (FCE).

The method is suitable for students of all nationalities, and ages. It requires no equipment (not even a whiteboard) or other books, and can be used for classes at private schools, state schools and universities. It is also possible for students to use the books to practise with each other when they are not at school.

In addition to this, students can practise their English online using the interactive exercises, which are available to students who study at licensed schools. Ask your school for details.

The Callan Method in practice

A Callan Method English lesson is probably very different from lessons you have done in the past. You do not sit in silence, doing a reading comprehension test or a grammar exercise from a book. You do not have 'free conversation', where you only use the English you already feel comfortable with. Of course, activities like this can help you, but you can do them at home with a book, or in a coffee bar. In a Callan Method lesson, you are busy with important activities that you cannot do outside the classroom. You are listening to English all the time. You are speaking English a lot, and all your mistakes are corrected. You learn quickly because you are always surrounded by English. There is no silence and no time to get bored or lose your concentration. And it is also fun!

So, what exactly happens in a Callan Method lesson, and how does it work?

The teacher asks you questions

The Callan Method books are full of questions. Each question practises a word, an expression, or a piece of grammar. The teacher is standing, and asks the questions to the students one by one. You never know when the teacher will ask you, so you are always concentrating. When one student finishes answering one question, the teacher immediately starts to ask the next question.

The teacher speaks quickly

The teacher in a Callan Method lesson speaks quickly. This is because, in the real world, it is natural to speak quickly. If you want to understand normal English, you must practise listening to quick natural speech and become able to understand English without first translating into your language. This idea of not translating is at the centre of the Callan Method; this method helps you to start thinking in English.

Also, we do not want you to stop and think a lot about the grammar while you are speaking. We want you to speak as a reflex, instinctively. And do not worry about mistakes. You will, naturally, make a lot of mistakes in the lessons, but Callan Method teachers correct your mistakes, and you learn from the corrections. When you go home, of course it will help if you read your book, think about the grammar, study the vocabulary, and do all the things that language students do at home – but the lessons are times to practise your listening and speaking, with your books closed!

The teacher says every question twice, and helps you with the answer

In the lesson, the teacher speaks quickly, so we say the questions twice. This way, you have another chance to listen if you did not understand everything the first time.

The teacher then immediately says the beginning of the answer. This is to help you (and 'push' you) to start speaking immediately. So, for example:

Teacher: *"Are there two chairs in this room? Are there two chairs in this room? No, there aren't ..."*

Student (immediately): *"No, there aren't two chairs in this room; there are twelve chairs in this room."*

If the teacher does not 'push' you by giving you the beginning of the answer, you might start to think too much, and translate into your language.

The teacher will speak along with you all the time while you are saying your answer. So, if you forget a word or you are not sure what to say, you will always hear the next word or two from the teacher. You should repeat after the teacher, but immediately try again to continue with the answer yourself. You must always try to continue speaking, and only copy the teacher when you cannot continue alone. That way, you will become more confident and learn more quickly. Never simply wait for help from the teacher and then copy – you will not improve so quickly.

Long answers, with the same grammar as the question

We want you to practise your speaking as much as possible, so you always make complete sentences when you speak in the lesson, using the same grammatical structure as in the question. For example:

Teacher: *"About how many pages are there in this book?"*

Student: *"There are about two hundred pages in that book."*

In this way, you are not just answering a question; you are making full sentences with the vocabulary and the grammar that you need to learn.

Correction by imitation

With the Callan Method, the teacher corrects all your mistakes the moment you make them. The teacher corrects you by imitating (copying) your mistake and then saying the correct pronunciation/form of the word. For example, if you say "He come from Spain", the teacher quickly says "not come - **comes**". This correction by imitation helps you to hear the difference between your mistake and the proper English form. You should immediately repeat the correct word and continue with your sentence. You learn a lot from this correction of your mistakes, and constant correction results in fast progress.

Contracted forms

In the lesson, the teacher uses contractions (e.g. the teacher says "I don't" instead of "I do not"). This is because it is natural to use contractions in spoken English and you must learn to understand them. Also, if you want to sound natural when you speak, you must learn to use contractions.

Lesson structure

Every school is different, but a typical 50-minute Callan lesson will contain about 35 minutes of speaking, a 10-minute period for reading, and a 5-minute dictation. The reading practice and the dictation are often in the middle of the lesson.

In the reading part, you read and speak while the teacher helps you and corrects your mistakes. In the dictation, you practise your writing, but you are also listening to the teacher. So, a 50-minute Callan lesson is 50 minutes of spoken English with no silence!

No chatting

Although the Callan Method emphasises the importance of speaking practice, this does not mean chatting (free conversation). You learn English quickly with the Callan Method partly because the lessons are organised, efficient, fast and busy. There is no time wasted on chatting; this can be done before or after the lesson.

Chatting is not a good way to spend your time in an English lesson. First, only some of the students speak. Second, in a chat, people only use the English that they already know. Third, it is difficult for a teacher to correct mistakes during a conversation.

The Callan Method has none of these problems. All through the lesson, every student is listening and speaking, practising different vocabulary and structures, and learning from the correction of their mistakes. And nobody has time to get bored!

Repeat, repeat, repeat!

Systematic revision

In your native language, you sometimes read or hear a word that you do not already know. You usually need to read or hear this new word only once or twice in order to remember it and then use it yourself. However, when you are learning a foreign language, things are very different. You need to hear, see and use words and grammatical structures many times before you really know them properly. So your studies must involve a system of revision (repeating what you have studied before). This is absolutely essential. If there is no system of revision in your studies, you will forget what you have studied and will not be able to speak or understand better than before.

In every Callan Method lesson, of course you learn new English, practise it, and progress through your book. However, you also do a lot of revision so that you can really learn what you have studied. Your teacher can decide how much revision your class needs, but it will always be an important part of your studies.

Also, because there is a lot of revision, it is not important for you to understand everything the first time; it gets easier. The revision with Callan is automatic and systematic. Every day you do a lot of revision and then learn some new English.

Revision in reading and dictation too

The reading and dictation practice in the lessons is part of Callan's systematic revision as well. First, you learn a new word in the speaking part of the lesson; a few lessons later, you meet it again when you are reading; finally, the word appears in a dictation. This is all written into the Callan Method; it happens automatically.

Correcting your dictations

With the Callan Method, there is little or no homework to do, but it is very important that you correct your dictations. These are printed in your book and so you can easily correct them at home, on the bus, or wherever. It is important to do this because it helps you to learn the written forms of the words you have already studied in earlier lessons.

Your first lessons with the Callan Method

During your first lesson with the Callan Method, all of the questions and some of the vocabulary are new for you; you have not done any revision yet. For this reason, the teacher may not ask you many questions. You can sit and listen, and become more familiar with the method - the speed, the questions, the correction etc.

History of the Callan Method – Robin Callan

Robin Callan is the creator of the Callan Method. He owns the Callan School in London's Oxford Street. He also runs Callan Publishing Limited, which supplies Callan Method books to schools all over the world.

Robin Callan grew up in Ely, Cambridgeshire, England. In his early twenties, he went to Italy to teach English in Salerno. Although he enjoyed teaching, Robin thought that the way in which teachers were expected to teach their lessons was inefficient and boring. He became very interested in the mechanisms of language learning, and was sure that he could radically improve the way English was taught.

He remained in Italy and started to write his own books for teaching English. He used these in his own classes and, over the following ten years, gained an immense amount of practical experience and a reputation for teaching English quickly and effectively.

When he returned to England, he opened his school in Oxford Street. As the method became more and more popular with students, the school grew and moved to larger premises. Robin continued to write his Callan Method books, and today the method is used by schools all over the world.

Robin Callan has always been passionate about English literature, especially poetry. For this reason, he bought The Orchard Tea Garden in Grantchester, near Cambridge, which attracts thousands of tourists each year. Throughout the 20th century, it was a popular meeting place for many famous Cambridge University students and important figures from English literature, such as Rupert Brooke, Virginia Woolf and E.M. Forster. Today, it is also home to the Rupert Brooke Museum.

Mr Callan now lives in Grantchester, but still plays an active role in the management of the Callan School in London.

The Callan School in London's Oxford Street

The largest private school in London

The Callan School in Oxford Street is the largest private school in London teaching English as a foreign language. Depending on the time of year, the school employs between 60 and 100 teachers and has an average of 1600 students passing through its doors every day. This number rises to more than 2000 in the middle of summer, similar to a small university.

Websites

Please visit the following websites for more information:

Callan Method http://www.callan.co.uk
Lots of information, including a list of schools around the world that use the method

Callan School London http://www.callanschoollondon.com/en/callan-school
All you need to know about the largest private English language school in London

How Callan Method Stages compare to CEFR* levels and University of Cambridge General English exams

Common European Framework of Reference

It is difficult to compare the Callan Method books directly with the CEFR levels and Cambridge exams, but below is an approximate guide.

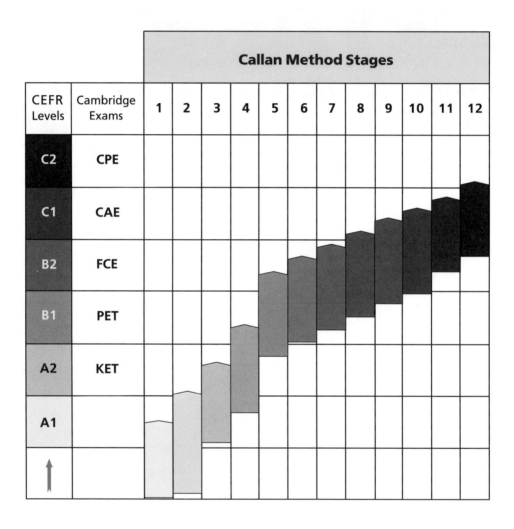

CEFR Levels	Cambridge Exams	Callan Method Stages											
		1	2	3	4	5	6	7	8	9	10	11	12
C2	CPE												
C1	CAE												
B2	FCE												
B1	PET												
A2	KET												
A1													

STAGE 6

LESSON 78

415 **situation**

What would you do if you saw someone taking something from a shop without paying? *If I saw ..., I'd ...*

What do people normally do in situations like that? *People normally ... in situations like that*

Do police officers often find themselves in dangerous situations? *Yes, police officers ...*

suppose   **thirst**

What do you suppose'd happen if there were suddenly no water in the world? *I suppose we'd all die of thirst if there ...*

If you only slept two hours tonight, how do you suppose you'd feel tomorrow morning? *If I only ..., I suppose I'd feel very tired tomorrow morning*

The word "supposing" can be used in a similar way to "if" when we want someone to imagine a particular situation. Therefore, we often use it in conditional sentences and say, for example, "Supposing you had no money, what would you do?"

Supposing today were Sunday, where'd you be now? *Supposing today were Sunday, I'd be ...*

Supposing you lost your passport, what would you do? *Supposing I lost my passport, I'd immediately tell the police*

416 **hotter and hotter**   **more and more**

Does it get hotter and hotter as we go towards the north of Europe? *No, it doesn't get ...; it gets colder and colder*

Do people usually become richer and richer as they become older? *Yes, people usually become ...*

Why? *Because they usually earn more and more money*

Does good wine usually become cheaper and cheaper as it becomes
older?   No, good wine doesn't ... ; it
usually becomes more and more expensive

ready   marriage

How long does it take you to get ready to go out in the morning?
                                        It takes me about ... to get ready to ...

When do you think you'll be ready to take the exam at the end of this
book?   I think I'll be ready ... in about ... weeks' time

Are you always ready to lend people money?   Yes, I'm always ...
                                              ~ No, I'm not always ...

Do you think most people are ready for marriage when they are eighteen
years old?   Yes, I think ... ~ No, I don't think ...

whereabouts

If the government of your country decided to build a new national sports
stadium, whereabouts do you think it should be?   If the government
of my country ..., I think ...

417 **describe**   **description**   **just**

Describe someone you know, please (one of your family or friends).
                                      I'll describe (my uncle: he's
tall and thin; he has black hair etc.)

Describe the place where you live.   The place where I live is
(by the sea; it's quite large; there
are some factories just outside it etc.)

What's he doing?   He's describing the place where he lives

Do you think it's a good enough description?   Yes, I think
it's ... ~ No, I don't think it's ...

correct   incorrect

Is it correct to say "The book was writing by him"?   No, it isn't ...; we
must say "The book was written by him"

Is it correct that 4 + 5 = 11?   No, it isn't ...; it's incorrect

as soon as   over

What did you do as soon as you came into the classroom?   I sat down
as soon as I ...

What'll you do as soon as the lesson is over?   I'll stand up,
go home etc. as soon as ...

418   When you lend something, like money for example, do you prefer the
other person to give it back on a certain date or just as soon as possible?

When I lend something ..., I prefer ...

strange

Who's the strangest person you know?   The strangest
person I know is ...

they = he or she

**We sometimes use the words "they", "them" etc. to talk about just
one person when we don't know if the person is a man or woman. For
example, "There is somebody in the next room and <u>they</u> are making a lot
of noise. I'm going to ask <u>them</u> to be quieter".**

When do we use the words "they", "them" etc. to talk about just one
person?   We use the words
"they", "them" etc. ... when we don't
know if the person is a man or woman

If someone lost their passport, what advice would you give them?
If someone lost <u>their</u> passport, I'd tell <u>them</u>
that <u>they</u> should immediately go to the police

shut   shut up   be quiet

**The verb "to shut up" means the same as "to be quiet" but is much less
polite, and we generally use it when we are angry.**

What verb can we use instead of the verb "to close"?   We can use the
verb "to shut" instead of ...

If some friends were talking loudly while you were trying to study, what
would you say?   If some ... while I was trying to study,
                                                         I'd say "Could you be quiet, please?"

419 And if they carried on talking loudly even after that, what might you then
     say?   If they ..., I might then say "Shut up!"

choose

Do you always choose your clothes yourself or does someone else ever
help you to choose them?   Yes, I always choose
                                                  my clothes myself ~ No, I don't always
                                        choose ... myself; sometimes someone helps me ...

If you had to choose between having £10,000 now or £40,000 in ten
years' time, which'd you choose?   If I had to choose
                                              between having ..., I'd choose ...

Why?

 *Dictation 49*

To cross the road/ without looking both ways/ would be very dangerous./ When
we say/ we should study,/ it means that we have an alternative,/ but that studying/
is the right thing to do;/ it is the best idea./ Although there were no bones/ in the
meat,/ it had been cooked/ so badly/ that it was impossible to eat./ English has its
origins/ in several other languages./ The war was directly caused/ by the actions of
the president.

 *Do Revision Exercise 32*

420 **recognize**

Do you think you'd be able to recognize me if we met each other again in thirty years' time?
Yes, I think I'd be able to recognize you if ... ~ No, I don't think I'd be able to recognize you if ...

Would you say you were good at recognizing people after not having seen them for several years?
Yes, I'd say I was good at ...
~ No, I wouldn't say I was good at ...

mas bien

rather

Would you say you spoke English rather well now?   Yes, I'd say I spoke ...

prefería

would rather

"Would rather" means the same as "would prefer". The difference is that we put the infinitive <u>without</u> "to" after "would rather", whereas we put the infinitive <u>with</u> "to" after "would prefer".

What can we say instead of "I would prefer to drink tea"?
We can say "I would rather drink tea" instead of "I would prefer to drink tea"

Would you rather have a cold drink than a hot drink at the moment?
Yes, I'd rather have ...
~ No, I wouldn't rather have ...

Which would you rather do this evening: read a book, watch television, or go to the cinema?
I'd rather ... than ...

421 Would you rather go on a long flight or a long train journey?
I'd rather ... than ...

faith   **Christian**

Do you have very much faith in your government?   Yes, I have a lot of faith in my government ~ No, I don't have very much faith in my government

About how old is the Christian faith?   The Christian faith is about two thousand years old

"Will" and "to be going to"

predict   **prediction**

just this moment

Two common ways to talk about the future are:

    I will go to London tomorrow (future simple)

    I am going to go to London tomorrow ("to be going to")

These different forms communicate different ideas.

One common use of the future simple is to communicate that we have <u>just this moment</u> decided to do something. For example, if I say "It's getting cold; I'll close the window", I am communicating that I have just this moment decided to close the window.

We can also use the future simple to make a prediction. For example, if I say to a friend "Don't worry about your exam tomorrow; I'm sure it will be easy", I am making a prediction that the exam will be easy.

422 Tell me one common use of the future simple, please.

                      One common use of the future simple is to communicate that we have just this moment decided to do something

Give me an example, please.   Sorry I forgot to bring the money for you; I'll bring it tomorrow, I promise!

Tell me another common use of the future simple, please.

                      Another common use of the future simple is to make a prediction

Give me an example, please.   I can't remember what she
                      looks like but I'm sure I'll recognize her when I see her

"To be going to" can also be used to make a prediction, but a prediction using information we already have. For example, if I say "Oh, look at the sky; I think it's going to rain", I am predicting rain because I can see that the sky is dark and cloudy now.

Another common use of "to be going to" is to communicate a future intention; something that we have <u>already</u> decided to do. For example, if I say "I'm going to buy a new car", I am communicating that I have already decided to buy a new car; it is my intention to buy one.

Tell me one common use of "to be going to", please.   One common
                          use of "to be going to" is to make a
                          prediction using information we already have

Give me an example, please.   Be careful; that wine glass
                                is going to fall off the table!

Tell me another common use of "to be going to", please.
                                Another common use of
                        "to be going to" is to communicate a future
                  intention; something that we have already decided to do

Give me an example, please.   I'm going to go to the
                                cinema next Saturday

423 **To communicate your future intentions, it is important to remember to use "to be going to", <u>not</u> the future simple. If you decide to watch a film tonight, and then later you tell a friend what you have decided to do, you should say "I'm going to watch a film tonight". It is wrong in this situation to say "I will watch a film tonight". This is a very common mistake.**

Tell me what you have decided to do this afternoon (or this evening),
please.   This afternoon (or this evening),
                                I'm going to visit a friend etc.

stairs	**upstairs**	**downstairs**
living room	**lift**	

In a house, are the bedrooms usually downstairs?   No, in a house ...;
                                they're usually upstairs

And is the living room usually upstairs?

No, the living room ...; it's usually downstairs

If you had to get to a room that was on the tenth floor of a building, would you take the stairs or the lift?

If I had to ..., I'd take the lift

lip **lipstick**

Is this my top lip?

No, it isn't your top lip; it's your bottom lip

Do you think women look better with or without lipstick?

I think women look ...

424 **system**

What system of government do you have in your country?

We have a ... system of government in my country

sail **sailor**

Is sailing a popular sport in your country?

Yes, sailing's ... in my country ~ No, sailing isn't ... in my country

Would you like to be a sailor?

Yes, I'd like to ... ~ No, I wouldn't like to ...

 *Dictation 50*

I do not get up/ immediately after I wake up,/ but I lie in bed/ for a few minutes./ We sometimes/ go through the summer/ without going for a swim./ There is no comparison/ between the prices on the website/ and those in the shop./ The fridge he bought/ from the shop on the corner/ was faulty./ It made him angry/ and he took a long time/ to calm down./ That guard dog/ is much too dangerous/ to keep in the house.

LESSON 80

425 **Emphatic "do"**   **deny**   **exclamation**   **stress**

I do speak English!   **I do like this book!**

As you already know, we use the auxiliary verb "do" for the present simple, but only in questions and negative sentences; it is not used in the positive. For example, we say "Do you speak English?" and "I do not speak English", but we say "I speak English", with no auxiliary "do".

However, when we want to be emphatic about something, we can also use "do" in a positive sentence. For example, if someone says to you "You don't speak English", you can reply "Yes I do speak English!" In situations like this, we put a heavy stress on the word "do".

When do we use the auxiliary verb "do" in a positive sentence with the present simple tense?

We use the ... when
we want to be emphatic

We usually use the emphatic "do" when we want to deny something that someone has said because we know it is not true. For example, if someone says to you "You don't eat healthy food", you can deny this strongly by saying "Yes I do eat healthy food!"

When do we usually use the emphatic "do"?

We usually use ...
when we want to deny something that
someone has said because we know it is not true

Give me an example, please.

For example, if somebody
says "You don't eat enough vegetables",
I can reply "Yes I do eat enough vegetables!"

426 Reply to this sentence using the emphatic form, please: you don't know what I've got in my pocket.

Yes I do know
what you've got in your pocket!

Another use of the emphatic "do" is in an exclamation. For example, "I do like this book!" and "He does speak good English!"

Tell me another use of the emphatic "do", please.

> Another use use ... is in an exclamation

Give me an example, please.

> I do hate noisy children! She does write beautifully!

Of course, we can use the emphatic "do" with the past simple too. For example, "I did study hard last year!" and "I did like that book you gave me!"

Reply to this sentence using the emphatic form in the past, please: He didn't cycle home yesterday.

> Yes he did cycle home yesterday!

Remember that we only use the emphatic "do" with the present and past simple. With other tenses, we just stress the first auxiliary verb, or the negative word in the verb. For example, "Yes I can speak English well!" and "No I won't make a mistake!"

Reply to these sentences using emphatic forms, please:

You can't read quickly.

> Yes I can read quickly!

The weather's been good.

> No the weather has not been good!

She doesn't love her family.

> Yes she does love her family!

He came to school early.

> No he didn't come to school early!

We shouldn't tell him the news.

> Yes we should tell him the news!

---

427   **hit**   **arrest**

What am I doing?

> You're hitting the table with your hand

Have you ever hit your head getting into a car?

> Yes, I've hit my head ... ~ No, I've never hit my head ...

What'd happen if you hit a policeman?

> If I hit a policeman, he'd arrest me

Have you ever seen anyone arrested?

> Yes, I've seen someone arrested ~ No, I've never seen anyone arrested

fair　　　　　　　　**fairly**　　　　　　　　**just**

feria, Exposición　　*bastante*
　　　　　　　　　justamente
　　　　　　　　　　　limpio

moderate　　　　　　　　**unfair**

injusto

The word "fair" has five different meanings, which are as follows: _____ (fair hair), _____ (industrial and agricultural fairs, for example), _____ (just), _____ (moderate), and _____ (fun fair).

What are the five meanings of the word "fair"?　　　The five meanings of
the word "fair" are ...

Do people become darker and darker in hair colour as we go towards the north of Europe?　　　No, people don't ...;
they become fairer and fairer

428　Have you ever been to an industrial or agricultural fair?　　　Yes, I've
been to ... ~ No, I've never been to ...

What kind?

If I asked everyone in this room twenty questions but only asked you two, would that be fair?　　　No, if you asked ...
but only asked me two, it
wouldn't be fair; it'd be unfair

Do they ever have a funfair in this town?　　　Yes, they sometimes have ...
~ No, they never have ...

Do you speak English fairly well now?　　　Yes, I speak
English fairly well now

pleasure

Is it a great pleasure for you to get up in the morning?　　　Yes, it's a great pleasure for me ...
~ No, it isn't a great pleasure for me ...

Why or why not?　　　Because I find my work interesting
~ Because, when I get up, it's often cold

Do you think it's possible for life to be full of pleasure all the time?　　　Yes, I think ... ~ No, I don't think ...

experiment

Do you think it's wrong to use animals for experiments?

Yes, I think it's ... ~ No, I don't think it's ...

429 discover

When was America discovered by Europeans, and who discovered it?

America was discovered
by Europeans in 1492 by Christopher
Columbus, or by Leif Ericsson about the year 1000

Is the internet useful for discovering new information?

Yes, the
internet ...

 *Do Revision Exercise 33*

LESSON 81

430 **scientist**

Would you like to be a scientist?

Yes, I'd like ...
~ No, I wouldn't like ...

Why or why not?

tissue

pañuelo.

What do we call a paper handkerchief?

We call a paper
handkerchief a tissue

division

How many football divisions are there in your country?

There are ...
football divisions in my country

Which division's your home town in?

My home town's
in the ... division

dentro

in **within** **on the other hand** *Por otra parte, de otra manera*

The time now is (6 o'clock). If I went out of the room and said to you "I'll be back in an hour's time", it would mean that I'd be back at (7 o'clock). If, on the other hand, I went out of the room and said "I'll be back within an hour", it'd mean that I'd be back at any time between now and (7 o'clock).

The time now is (6 o'clock). If I went out of the room and said "I'll be back in an hour", at what time would I return?

If you went ...,
you'd return at (7 o'clock)

431 If, on the other hand, I went out of the room and said "I'll be back within an hour", at what time would I return?

If, on the other hand,
you went ..., you'd return at any
time between now and (7 o'clock)

Do you think life will be discovered on other planets within the next hundred years?

Yes, I think ... ~ No, I don't think ...

main   mainly   shopping

Which is the main shopping street in this town?

... is the main shopping ...

Do you think that the difference between the people of one country and those of another is mainly a question of language?

Yes, I think ...
~ No, I don't think ...

sing – sang – sung

What are the three forms of "sing"?

The three forms of "sing" are "sing, sang, sung"

Why are people so often in the habit of singing to themselves in the bathroom?

People are so often ... maybe because their voices sound better in the bathroom

If you sang in public for a day (in the street, for example), how much do you think you'd earn?

If I sang in public for a day, I think I'd earn about ...

Have you ever sung in public?

Yes, I've ... ~ No, I've never ...

432   profit   loss   business

If you bought a business for £1,000,000 and sold it again later for £250,000, would you be making a profit?

No, if I bought ..., I wouldn't be making a profit; I'd be making a loss

How much would your loss be?

My loss'd be £750,000

Future perfect   I will have eaten

We use the future perfect when we are thinking about time before and up to a specific point in the future. For example, if you know that you will be in bed at midnight tonight, you can tell a friend "Please don't phone me at midnight; I will have gone to bed". This communicates that you will go to bed before midnight and that, at midnight, you will be in bed, probably sleeping.

When do we use the future perfect?

We use the future perfect when we are thinking about time before and up to a specific point in the future

Give me an example, please

When you arrive at my house, I will have cooked dinner

What does that sentence mean?

That sentence means that I will finish cooking dinner before you arrive at my house; when you arrive, dinner will be ready

433 Tell me the difference between these two sentences:

"At 9 o'clock, I will eat my dinner"

and

"At 9 o'clock, I will have eaten my dinner".

The difference ... is that "At 9 o'clock, I will eat my dinner" means I will start to eat my dinner at 9 o'clock, whereas "At 9 o'clock, I will have eaten my dinner" means that my dinner will already be finished at 9 o'clock

Will you have had your dinner before midnight tonight?

Yes, I'll have had my ... ~ No, I won't have had my ...

Will we have left this room in three hours' time?

Yes, we'll have left ... ~ No, we won't have left ...

At 10 o'clock tomorrow morning, will you already have got up?

Cet,ar
↑

Yes, at ..., I'll already have got up ~ No, at ..., I won't already have got up

Will most shops in this town have shut before eleven o'clock this evening?

Yes, most shops in this town will have shut ...

minister   prime

What's a government minister?

A government minister is someone who has a very important job in the government

Give me some examples, please.

Minister for Agriculture, Foreign Minister etc.

What do some countries call the most important minister in the government?

Some countries call ... the Prime Minister

adivinor-

434 guess

Are you usually able to guess a person's age?

Yes, I'm usually ... ~ No, I'm not usually ...

coin

Have you got any coins in your pocket (or bag) at the moment?

Yes, I've got some ... ~ No, I haven't got any ...

Cheers!

In which situations do we say "Cheers!"?
We say "Cheers!" to express good wishes when we have a drink with somebody, to say "thank you", and to say "goodbye"

 Dictation 51

In some countries,/ a lot of things used daily/ belong to the government,/ such as the roads,/ the trains, water and electricity./ The notice/ outside the building/ said that the man was wanted/ dead or alive./ Don't throw/ that piece of paper away;/ I still need it./ I haven't finished with it yet./ The little boy/ had just been given a tissue/ by his mother,/ but he immediately dropped it/ on the floor/ and made it dirty./ He sat on his own/ during the flight.

LESSON 82

....

435 **rode**

Cabalgar → Past

What's the past of "ride"? The past of "ride" is "rode"

If you rode from here to the next town by bicycle, about how long would it take you? If I rode ..., it'd take me about ...

decrease

Does the temperature decrease as we move from spring to summer?
No, the temperature doesn't decrease ...; it increases

Conjunto
mixto
unido

join **joint** *mutuo* *hombro* **shoulder** *codo* **elbow**

Do you have to join a library before you can start borrowing books?
Yes, you have to ...

If we join two pieces of wood together like this, what do we make?
If we join ... like that, we make a cross

What joint of the arm is this? That joint ... is the shoulder, the elbow, the wrist

436 **noon**

What's another word for midday? Another word for midday is noon

e.g. = exempli gratia = for example

abbreviation

The letters "e.g." are the abbreviation of "exempli gratia", from the Latin, which means "for example". We use these letters in writing, but not in speaking.

What are the letters "e.g." the abbreviation of? The letters "e.g." are ...

When do we use these letters? We use these letters …

here you are **there he is**

hand **structure** **finally**

aquí Están

We use the expression **"Here you are"** when we hand something to somebody. For example, if you say **"Can I borrow your book, please?"**, I can reply **"Yes, of course you can; here you are"**.

What can we say when we hand something to somebody?

When we …, we can say "Here you are"

We also use this same structure with the words **"here"** or **"there"** in other situations. For example, when we are trying to find a particular person and we suddenly see them, we can say **"Ah, here you are!"**, or when we are pointing somebody out in a photograph, we can say **"There he is"**.

437 When you finally find something after trying to find it for a long time, what can you say?

When you finally …, you can say "Ah, here it is!"

Estado / Condición *Rellenar*

state **fill in** **application form**

birth **occupation**

Do you pay taxes to the state? Yes, I pay … ~ No, I don't pay …

Is this room in a good state or a bad state? This room's in a … state

When you fill in a passport application form, what must you state?

When I fill in …, I must state my name, my address, my date of birth, my occupation etc.

declaración

statement **signature**

When you make a formal written statement to the police, do you have to put your signature at the end? Yes, when you make …, you have to …

download   **program**

What kind of things can we download from the internet?   We can
                                                            download programs, songs, films ...

438   **drunk**   **fight**

What happens if someone drinks too much alcohol?   If someone ... ,
                                                            they get drunk

Have you ever seen two people fighting each other in the street?
                                                            Yes, I've seen ...
                                                        ~ No, I've never seen ...

Where? What happened?

Do some people get into fights when they're drunk?   Yes, some
                                                            people ...

probability

Do you think the probability of another world war has increased or
decreased in the last twenty years?   I think the
                                        Cambiar de opinion   probability of ...

mind   **brain**   *C*   **change one's mind**

brainy   **abstract**   **sense**

**We use "mind" in the abstract sense, whereas we generally use "brain" in
the physical sense.**

What's the difference between "mind" and "brain"?   The difference
                                            between "mind" and "brain" is that we use ...

Are you in the habit of changing your mind a lot?
                                    Yes, I'm in the habit of changing my mind a lot
                                ~ No, I'm not in the habit of changing my mind a lot

Do adults have bigger brains than young children?   Yes, adults have ...

439   Who's the brainiest member of your family?   My ... is the brainiest
                          ↓   member of my family

          mas inteligente.

criminal

What happens to criminals if the police catch them?

If the police catch criminals, they arrest them and take them to the police station

gun

Do you have to have permission from the state to own a gun in your country?

Yes, you have to have ... in my country

civilized

Do you think the world's more civilized nowadays than it was in the past?

Yes, I think ... ~ No, I don't think ...;
I think it's less civilized

so far

How many people do you think you've spoken to so far today?

I think I've spoken to about ...

What does the expression "so far, so good" mean?

The expression "so far, so good" means that somebody has not experienced any problems up to now

Give me an example, please.

I'm enjoying my new job; so far, so good!

Do Revision Exercise 34

LESSON 83

<u>**Short answers with auxiliary verbs**</u>

Yes, I can   **Yes, I would**   **Yes, I am**

Yes, I have   **Yes, I do**

We can give short answers to questions simply by using an auxiliary verb.

For example: **"Can you speak Spanish?"**   **"Yes, I can."**

"Have you seen David?"   **"No, I haven't."**

"Will she be working?"   **"Yes, she will."**

en lugar de

Notice that only the first auxiliary verb is necessary. Instead of "Yes, she will be", we can just say "Yes, she will".

Answer the following questions with short answers:

Will we still be here in two minutes' time?   Yes, we will

Would you need any money if you went to the cinema and had a free ticket?   No, I wouldn't

Can you swim?   Yes, I can ~ No, I can't

Should you be very careful when you cross the road?   Yes, you should

Could you read when you were three years old?   Yes, I could ~ No, I couldn't

441   **We can also make short answers with the verbs "be" and "have".**

For example: **"Are you a student?"**   **"Yes, I am."**

"Has he got the money?"   **"Yes, he has."**

Am I the teacher?   Yes, you are

Have you got any shoes on your feet?   Yes, I have

For short answers with the present simple and past simple, we use the auxiliary "do".

For example: **"Does he eat meat?"**   **"Yes, he does."**

                        "Did they finish the job?"   **"No, they didn't."**

Do you like this part of the country?   Yes, I do ~ No, I don't

Did you eat dinner at home last night?   Yes, I did ~ No, I didn't

Does he/she speak his/her language during the lesson?   No, he/she
                                                                    doesn't

Did people believe the world was round in the old days?   No, they didn't

Of course, we don't use short answers in the lessons because it's important for you to practise speaking as much as possible.

Why don't we use short answers in the lessons?   We don't use ...
                                                    because it's important for us
                                              to practise speaking as much as possible

leuen lavse

rose

What's the past of "rise"?   The past of "rise" is "rose"

Did the sun rise early this morning?   Yes, the sun rose ...
                                                    ~ No, the sun didn't rise ...

442 **how high**   **mile**   **(decimal) point**

kilometre   **population**

About how high are the walls of this room in feet?   The walls of this
                                                room are about ... feet high

About how long is this table in feet?   This table is
                                                about ... feet long

If I am (5) feet (11) inches tall, about how tall do you think you are in feet
and inches?   If you are ..., I think I'm
                                                about ... feet ... inch(es) tall

There are about 1.6 (one point six) kilometres in a mile.

About how many kilometres are there in a mile?   There are
                                                        about 1.6 kilometres in a mile

A kilometre equals about 0.6 (point six) of a mile.

If a kilometre equals about 0.6 (point six) of a mile, how far is it from here
to the nearest town in miles?   If a kilometre ...,
                                            it's about ... mile(s) from here to ...

What's the population of this town?   The population
dano   _falav_   of this town is about ...
                                            caerse
443   **hurt – hurt – hurt**   **fell**   **fall over**

What's the past of "fall"?   The past of "fall" is "fell"

If you fell over while you were running along the street, might you hurt
yourself?   Yes, if I fell over while I was running
                                            along the street, I might hurt myself

Have you ever been hurt while playing sport?   Yes, I've
                                            been ... ~ No, I've never been ...

If you hurt yourself very badly, where'd you be taken to?   If I hurt
                                    myself very badly, I'd be taken to hospital

glad

Would you be glad to hear that you had failed an exam?   No, I
                                            wouldn't be glad to hear
                                            that I'd ...; I'd be very unhappy

Would you be glad if you were told you had won the lottery?
                                    Yes, I'd be glad if I were told I'd ...
enfermo   _enfermo_
sick   **unwell**   **vomit**

What are two other words for "ill"?   Two other words
                                    for "ill" are "sick" and "unwell"

**"To be sick" can mean "to be unwell", but it can also mean "to vomit". We
usually understand the meaning from the sentence or situation.**

What's another meaning of "to be sick" besides "to be unwell"?
                                    Another meaning of ... is "to vomit"

444 What does this sentence probably mean: "The little boy was sick in the
car"?

> That sentence probably means
> that the little boy vomited in the car

What does this sentence probably mean: "The little boy didn't go to
school because he was sick"?

> That sentence probably
> means that the little boy didn't
> go to school because he was unwell

repair

When things break, do you normally try to repair them or do you just
throw them away?

> When things break, I normally ...

techo
roof

What do we call the top covering of a house?

> We call ... the roof

wind   windy

navegar
Do sailing boats move faster in strong winds?

> Yes, sailing boats ...

ventoso
Is it a windy day today?

> Yes, it's a ... ~ No, it isn't a ...

Capturado   *Asi como*
caught   just as   platform

coger
What are the three forms of "catch"?

> The three forms
> of "catch" are "catch, caught, caught"

When was the last time you caught a cold?

> The last time
> I caught a cold was ....

445 Have you ever caught a train just as it was leaving the platform?

> Yes, I've sometimes caught ...
> ~ No, I've never caught ...

Dictation 52 .... *inutil* ....

In the old days,/ people were very much afraid/ of their kings./ It is useless/ thinking
about what will happen/ if they win,/ simply because they won't win./ My pen is
the most useful thing/ that I possess./ Mix some wine with it,/ add some ice from
the freezer,/ and then pour the lot/ into a large glass./ The two countries/ wouldn't
even unite/ to protect themselves/ against their common enemy./ We chatted
online/ until after midnight.

446 **Direct speech and indirect speech**

comillas

report   **refer**   **inverted commas**

Direct speech: I said "The room is large"

Indirect speech: I said that the room was large

There are two ways in which we can repeat what someone has said. We can use direct speech, and <u>give the exact words</u> of the speaker, like this:

Mr Brown said "I like warm weather".

We can also use indirect speech, and <u>report</u> what Mr Brown said, like this:

Mr Brown said that he liked warm weather.

Notice that indirect speech is also called reported speech.

What are the two ways in which we can repeat what someone has said?

> The two ways ... are by giving the exact words of the speaker, or by reporting what the speaker said

What do we call these two ways?

> We call these two ways direct speech and indirect speech

Give me an example of direct speech, please.

> Mr Brown said "I like warm weather"

Give me an example of indirect speech, please.

> Mr Brown said that he liked warm weather

447 **When we change direct speech into indirect speech, we generally move the verb into the past, or further into the past. For example, we change present tenses into past tenses.**

For example: (Direct speech)   The teacher said "The room is large".

(Indirect speech)   The teacher said that the room was large.

(Direct speech)   The teacher said "I have drunk the coffee".

(Indirect speech)   The teacher said that he had drunk the coffee.

If a verb is already in the past, it often remains unchanged. However, sometimes we put it further into the past so the exact meaning is easier to understand. Think about this sentence:

Mary said that she went to the cinema.

Here, we don't know whether Mary said "I go to the cinema" or "I went to the cinema". In other words, we don't know if she was speaking about a habit in the present or a single visit in the past. However, we could say this instead:

Mary said that she <u>had been</u> to the cinema.

Now it becomes clearer that she was speaking about a single visit in the past.

What do we do with the tenses when we change direct speech into indirect speech?

When we change ..., we generally move the verb into the past

Give me an example.

The teacher said "The room is large".
The teacher said that the room was large.

What do we do if a verb is already in the past?

If a verb ...,
it often remains unchanged, but
sometimes we put it further into the past

448 **In indirect speech, the word "will" changes to "would". We use "would" when we are speaking about the past but want to refer to a future action.**

For example: (Direct speech)   Mary said "John will go to London".

(Indirect speech)   Mary said that John would go to London.

You are reporting what Mary said in the past, but the word "would" refers to a future action.

What do we do with the word "will" when we change direct speech into indirect speech?   When we change ..., we change the word "will" to "would"

Give me an example, please.   She said that John would go to London next year

Right. I will now make some statements and I want you to tell me what I said, using indirect speech.

"I swim every day" – What did I say?   You said that you swam every day

"She is speaking to you" – What did I say?   You said that she was speaking to me

"I have just taken the pen from the table" – What did I say?   You said that you had just taken the pen from the table

"I think I will go to London tomorrow" – What did I say?   You said that you thought you would go to London tomorrow

"They had books in their hands when they came into the room" – What did I say?   You said that they had books in their hands when they came into the room

"I ate too much for dinner" – What did I say?   You said you had eaten too much for dinner

449 **Notice that words like "I", "you", "my", "your" etc. sometimes need to change when direct speech becomes indirect speech.**

Notice also that for indirect speech we do not use inverted commas, and it is not generally necessary to use the word "that" to connect the two parts of the sentence.

Do we use inverted commas for indirect speech?   No, we don't use ...

Is it generally necessary to use the word "that" when we use indirect speech?   No, it isn't ...

Give me an example, please.   He said <u>that</u> the room was large ~ He said the room was large

flat

Did people in the old days believe the world was round?   No, people ...; they believed it was flat

Which is one of the flattest parts of this country?   One of the flattest parts of this country is ...

pity   what a pity   picnic   phrase

Would you think it was a great pity if you went for a picnic in the country and it rained?   Yes, I'd think ... if I ...

What kind of people do you pity most?   I pity ... most

Translate this phrase: "What a pity".

450 blow – blew – blown

What are the three forms of "blow"?   The three forms of "blow" are "blow, blew, blown"

Have you ever been blown off your feet by the wind?
        Yes, I've been blown off my feet by the wind
        ~ No, I've never been blown off my feet by the wind

 *Dictation 53*

Please leave your dirty plates/ in the sink./ The teacher told the girl's mother/ that he found the girl's school studies/ were not as good as/ they should be./ They would rather live/ in an agricultural region/ of the country/ than a crowded city./ The actress made no apology/ for her lateness./ Customers in a shop/ are called "sir" or "madam",/ and an officer is called "sir"/ by his men./ My colleague takes great care of his car/ and lets no one else use it.

 Do Revision Exercise 35

LESSON 85

451 **consider**   **decision**

What do you consider to be the best occupation in the world?

> I consider ... to be the
> best occupation in the world

Why must we consider carefully before making an important decision?

> We must ... because, if we don't consider
> carefully, we might make a big mistake

whatever   **whenever**   **wherever**

[handwritten: cualquier. a cosa, cuando quiera, siempre que, donde quiera]

whoever   **limit**   **unlimited**

[handwritten: cualquiera]

most of → *[handwritten: la mayor parte.]*

The difference between the words "what" and "whatever" is that we use the word "what" in a limited sense, whereas we use the word "whatever" in a more unlimited sense. Other examples of this kind of thing are: "when – whenever"; "where – wherever"; "who – whoever".

What's the difference between the words "what" and "whatever"?

> The difference between ... is that
> we use the word "what" in a limited sense, whereas
> we use the word "whatever" in a more unlimited sense

If you could buy whatever you wanted, what would you buy?

> If I could buy whatever I wanted, I'd buy ...

Can you go for a holiday whenever you like?

> Yes, I can
> go for a holiday whenever I like
> ~ No, I can't go for a holiday whenever I like

452 Why or why not?   Because I have to work (or study) for most of the year

If you could go wherever you liked in the world, where'd you go?

> If I could go wherever I liked in the world, I'd go to ...

If you could meet whoever you wanted in the world, who would you prefer to meet?

> If I could meet whoever
> I wanted in the world, I'd prefer to meet ...

mentir   _decir la verdad_   _mentir_

truth	lie	tell the truth	tell a lie

honest

Do you always tell the truth?

> Yes, I always …
> ~ No, I don't always …; sometimes I tell lies

Why or why not?

> Because I think it's important
> to be honest ~ Because it's sometimes
> necessary to tell lies in order not to be unpleasant

Do newspapers always tell the truth?

> No, newspapers
> don't …; sometimes they tell lies

Why do they sometimes tell lies?

> They sometimes tell lies because …

miss

What's the opposite of the verb "to catch"?

> The opposite … is "to miss"

If I threw my pen to you, do you think you'd catch it or miss it?

> If you threw your pen to me, I think I'd …

Are you in the habit of missing trains and buses?

> Yes, I'm in the
> habit … ~ No, I'm not in the habit …

453 Why or why not?

> Because I always leave everything to the
> last minute and then have to hurry ~ Because I
> always give myself plenty of time to catch trains and buses

How long do you have to be away from home before you begin to miss your family and friends?

> I have to be away from home for
> about … before I begin …

Did you miss the last lesson?

> Yes, I missed …
> ~ No, I didn't miss …

If so, why?

union	trade union	organization

in favour of	pay (wages)

Do you think that a union of all the countries in Europe (or South America etc.) will ever be possible?

> Yes, I think … will
> one day be possible ~ No, I
> don't think … will ever be possible

What is a trade union?　　　　　　A trade union is an organization composed
of workers from a particular industry. It protects
the workers and fights to improve their pay and conditions

Are you in favour of trade unions?　　　　　　　　Yes, I'm in favour ...
~ No, I'm not in favour ...

rope　　　　　　　　　　**climb**

What can we use rope for?　　　　　　　　We can use rope for
climbing mountains, pulling things etc.

454 What'd you see if you climbed the stairs to the top of this building?
If I climbed ..., I'd see ...

Is it easy to climb to the top of the music industry and stay there?
No, it isn't easy ...; it's difficult

court　　　　　　　　　**look for**

If you lost your keys, where would you look for them first?　　If I lost my
keys, I would ...

Where do people go when they are looking for justice?　　People go
to the law courts when they ...

judge

Would you like the job of a judge?　　Yes, I'd like ... ~ No, I wouldn't like ...

dark – darken　　　　　　**short – shorten**

wide – widen – width　　　　**length – lengthen**

strength – strengthen　　　　**friendship**

**We can form verbs from certain adjectives or nouns by adding the letters
"en". For example, from the adjective "dark" we can make the verb
"to darken", which means "to make darker" or "to get darker". Other
examples are "short – shorten", "wide – widen" etc.**

How do we form verbs from certain adjectives or nouns?　　We form
verbs from certain ... by adding the letters "en"

Give me some examples, please.   dark – darken;
                                                              short – shorten etc.

455 What does the verb "to darken" mean?   The verb"to darken"
                                                means "to make darker" or "to get darker"

If our trousers are too long, what must we do to them?
                                          If our trousers ..., we must shorten them

Do the days lengthen or shorten as we go towards summer?
                                                   The days lengthen as we ...

Do you think sport can strengthen the friendship between different
countries?   Yes, I think ... ~ No, I don't think ...

**An adjective or noun must have only one syllable in order for us to form a
verb from it. There are also some one-syllable adjectives and nouns from
which we cannot form a verb. We can't say, for example, "to smallen"; we
say "to make smaller".**

How many syllables must an adjective or noun have in order for us to
form a verb from it?   An adjective or noun must
                                     have only one syllable in order for us ...

Can we form verbs from all adjectives and nouns of one syllable?
                                                   No, we can't form verbs ...

Give me an example of a one-syllable adjective from which we can't form
a verb?   An example of a ... is "small"
                                                   (or "large", "slow" etc.)

 *Dictation 54*

When we hurry,/ we are not able to do things/ as well as/ when we take our time./
You can eat/ as much as you like;/ we've got plenty of sandwiches,/ crisps and
biscuits./ I haven't eaten so much chocolate/ since I was a little boy./ We were
late/ for an appointment with our boss,/ and so we had to run./ If I lend you some
money,/ will you pay it back/ when promised?/ One should not make important
decisions,/ especially about one's career,/ without thinking carefully.

456 **obvious**

Give me a sentence with the word "obvious". It is obvious from what he says that he is not interested in the job

Do small children sometimes say they aren't tired when they obviously are? Yes, small children sometimes ...

Why? Because they don't want to go to bed etc.

ache	toothache	stomach ache

earache	headache

An ache is a continuous physical pain, such as toothache, headache, stomach ache, earache etc.

What is an ache? An ache is a continuous ...

What might you get if you ate too much? I might get stomach ache if I ...

Where should you go if you get toothache? I should go to the dentist's if I ...

What kind of things give you a headache? The kind of things that give me a headache are noise, too much work, hot weather etc.

rule	confuse

Who was the last person to rule your country ? ... was the last person to rule my country

457 Do you understand the rules of football? Yes, I understand ... ~ No, I don't understand ...

Do the rules of English grammar sometimes confuse you? Yes, the rules of English grammar sometimes confuse me

Do you find computers confusing?

Yes, I find …
~ No, I don't find …

Would you be confused if I suddenly walked out of the room for no reason and didn't come back?

Yes, I'd be confused if you …

ought

"Ought" has the same meaning as "should", but it must be followed by the infinitive with "to". For example, instead of saying "I should go now", we say "I ought to go now". In normal everyday conversation, "should" is more common than "ought".

What can we say instead of "should"?

We can say "ought" …

Give me an example, please.

I ought to call my dad because it's his birthday

When we borrow money, ought we to pay it back as soon as possible?

Yes, when we …, we ought to …

What ought we to do before crossing the road?

We ought to look both ways before …

Do you think children ought to be allowed to go to bed whenever they want?

No, I don't think children ought to …

458 **rough**   **smooth**   **surface**   **seasick**

roughly

Is the surface of this table rough?

No, the surface …; it's smooth

When we speak about the sea, we usually describe it as "calm" instead of "smooth".

When you travel by boat, do you prefer the sea to be rough?

No, when I travel by boat, I don't …; I prefer it to be calm

Why?

Because a rough sea makes me feel seasick …

If someone tells you that they're feeling rough, what do they mean?

If someone tells me …, they mean they aren't feeling very well

Roughly how many people would you say there were in Spain (or Russia, China etc.)? I'd say there were roughly ...

Do you like rough weather? Yes, I like rough weather ~ No, I don't like rough weather; I prefer calm weather

Which do you think is the roughest sport one can play? I think maybe rugby is the roughest ...

459 **ground**   **level**   **underground**

railway   **ground floor**   **grounds**

By the word "ground", we usually mean the surface of the land.

What do we usually mean by the word "ground"? By the word "ground", we usually ...

Are there any shops in this town built below the level of the ground (or ground level)? Yes, there are some ... ~ No, there aren't any ...

Where?

When a table is not level, what must we do? When a table ..., we must put something under one of its legs

Has this town got an underground railway? Yes, this town's got ... ~ No, this town hasn't got ...

What's on the ground floor of this building? There's (or there are) ... on the ground floor of this building

Where's the biggest football ground in this town? The biggest football ground in this town is ...

Are the grounds of some famous old buildings in this country open to the public? Yes, the grounds ...

educate   **educated**

How can parents start educating their children before they go to school? Parents can ... by teaching them to read and write etc.

460 What do we mean by an educated person? By an educated person, we mean somebody who has continued their studies to a high level

Making a suggestion

Here are four common ways in which we can make a suggestion:

1) Shall we go to the cinema?

2) Let's go to the cinema.

3) How (or What) about going to the cinema?

4) Why don't we go to the cinema?

Tell me four common ways in which we can make a suggestion, please.

Four common ways in which we can make a suggestion are:
1) Shall we wait for him?
2) Let's wait for him.
3) How (or What) about waiting for him?
4) Why don't we wait for him?

The imperative — order

When we want to say something stronger than just a suggestion, or even order someone to do something, we use the imperative. In English, the imperative is very easy; we just use the infinitive without "to". For example, we say "Go away!" For a negative imperative, we put the word "don't" before the infinitive. For example, we say "Don't go away!"

How do we make the imperative in English?

We make the imperative in English by using the infinitive without "to"

Give me some examples, please.

Give me the book! Do it now! Have a nice day!

461 How do we make a negative imperative?

We make a negative imperative by putting the word "don't" before the infinitive

Give me some examples, please.

Don't give him the book! Don't be late! Don't forget to email me!

Do Revision Exercise 36

LESSON 87

462 **overeat**   **oversleep**   **overwork**

overcook   **undercook**   **overpay**   **underpay**

When we put the word "over" before a verb, it sometimes means to do something excessively.

What does it sometimes mean when we put the word "over" before a verb?

> When we put the word "over" before a verb, it sometimes means ...

Give me some examples, please.

> oversleep; overeat etc.

What might happen if we overate?

> If we overate, we might get stomach ache

Have you ever been late for work (or school) because you've overslept?

> Yes, I've ... ~ No, I've never ...

Are nurses and doctors in busy hospitals often overworked?

> Yes, nurses and doctors ...

Some verbs, like "overcook" or "overpay", form their opposite with the word "under" – e.g. "undercook", "underpay".

What are the contraries of "overcook" and "overpay"?

> The contraries of "overcook" and "overpay" are "undercook" and "underpay"

What do we mean when we say that somebody is underpaid for the work they do?

> When we say that ..., we mean they are not paid enough for the work they do

463 **charge**   **serious**   **commit**   **battery**

service

What happens to people who are charged by the police with committing serious crimes?

> People who are charged ... are first taken to court, and then, if they are found guilty, they are sent to prison

How would you feel if you were told to charge the enemy in a battle?

If I were told …, I'd probably feel very afraid

If you had to be in charge of a big business, what kind of business would you choose?

If I had to …, I'd choose …

If you were seriously overcharged in a restaurant, would you ask to speak to the manager?

Yes, if I were …, I'd ask to …

Have you ever refused to pay the service charge in a restaurant?

Yes, I've … ~ No, I've never …

Another use of the word "charge" is in charging a battery, for example in a mobile phone.

What's another use of the word "charge"?

Another use …

How often do you have to recharge your mobile?

I have to recharge my mobile …

clear	as regards	

Was the sky clear yesterday?

Yes, the sky was …
~ No, the sky wasn't …

464 Can you make yourself clearly understood when you speak English in everyday situations?

Yes, I can make myself clearly understood when I …

At what time of day are the streets usually at their clearest as regards traffic?

The streets are usually …

Who clears the tables in a restaurant?

The waiters and waitresses clear …

guest	host/hostess	invite

anfitrión   anfitriona

If you invited me to your house, would you be my guest or my host/hostess?

If I invited you to my house, I'd be your host/hostess

If you could play host to three famous guests, which three famous people would you choose?

If I could play…,
I'd choose …

ridden

What are the three forms of "ride"?

> The three forms
> of "ride" are "ride, rode, ridden"

Have you ever ridden a horse?

> Yes, I've ridden ...
> ~ No, I've never ridden ...

Have you ever ridden a bicycle at night without lights?

> Yes, I've ...
> ~ No, I've never ...

465 severe

If you were a judge, on what kind of criminals would you be most severe?

> If I were a judge, the kind of
> criminals I'd be most severe on would be ...

Do you get very severe winters in your country?

> Yes, we get ...
> ~ No, we don't get ...

blow

What do people say they see when they receive a blow on the head?

> People say they see stars when ...

respect

What kind of people do you respect most?

> The kind of
> people I respect most are ...

company   employ   employer   employee

If you had your own company, would you employ someone simply because they were a friend?

> Yes, if I had my
> own company, I'd ... ~ No, if I
> had my own company, I wouldn't ...

What do we employ to cut bread?

> We employ a
> knife to cut bread

What do we call a person who employs somebody to work for them?

> We call ... an "employer"

And what do we call the person who works for them?

> We call ... an
> "employee"

Are there a lot of machines in a factory?

Yes, there are ...

What do we use a cash machine for?

We use a cash
machine for taking money
out of the bank quickly and easily

What could happen if you accidentally put a red sock in a washing
machine with white clothes?

If I accidentally ...,
I could get pink clothes

flown

What are the three forms of "fly"?

The three forms of
"fly" are "fly, flew, flown"

Have you ever flown in a plane?

Yes, I've ... ~ No, I've never ...

draw   drawing   curtain

**The verb "to draw" means to make a picture with a pencil or pen. It can
also mean "to pull". For example, if you draw the curtains, you pull them
open or closed. If you draw money from the bank, you put your bank card
in a cash machine and take money out.**

Are you good at drawing pictures?

Yes, I'm ... ~ No, I'm not ...

What do we mean by a rough drawing?

By a rough drawing, we
mean a very simple drawing

What's the easiest way to draw out cash?

The easiest way ... is to use a
bank card in a cash machine

What does "to draw the curtains" mean?

"To draw the curtains" means
to pull them open or closed

  *Dictation 55*

All right,/ but the root of the problem/ still remains./ When a man murders another
man,/ ought we to put him in prison/ or kill him?/ It's difficult to cross the road/ in
safety nowadays./ He lay down quietly/ with his head on the pillow/ and went to
sleep./ Your idea sounds exciting./ When we get wet,/ we have to take our clothes
off/ and dry them./ I've put your cheese/ in the fridge./ In spite of the fact that/ he
looks quite tall,/ he is only average height.

468 **Perfect continuous**

Present participle   **if ... then ...**

We form the perfect continuous tenses by using the verb "have", the word "been" and the present participle of the main verb.

Present perfect continuous: I <u>have</u> been working

Past perfect continuous: I <u>had</u> been working

Future perfect continuous: I <u>will have</u> been working

How do we form the perfect continuous tenses?   We form ... by using the verb "have", the word "been", and the present participle of the main verb

Give me an example, please.   I have been studying for two hours

We use the present perfect continuous to say how long an action has been in progress so far. We are "measuring" the duration of the action up to now. For example, if you arrive at work at 9 a.m., then at 10 a.m. you can say "I have been working for one hour so far"; later, at 11 a.m., you can say "I have been working for two hours so far".

When do we use the present perfect continuous?   We use the present perfect continuous to say how long an action has been in progress so far

Give me an example, please.   I have been living in this house for six months so far

469 **We use the past perfect continuous to communicate the duration of an action up to a particular point in the past. We are "measuring" how long the action had already been in progress at that point. For example, the sentence "I had been cooking for twenty minutes when she arrived" means that I started cooking and then twenty minutes later she arrived.**

When do we use the past perfect continuous? We use the past perfect continuous to communicate the duration of an action up to a particular point in the past

Give me an example, please. I had been living in this house for one month when I bought my new bed

We use the future perfect continuous to communicate the duration of an action up to a particular point in the future. For example, "At the end of this lesson, we will have been studying for ... minutes".

When do we use the future perfect continuous? We use the future perfect continuous to communicate the duration of an action up to a particular point in the future

Give me an example, please. I will have been living in this house for eight months at the end of this year

How long had you been sitting in this room for when I came in? I had been sitting in this room for ... when you came in

Since when have you been studying English? I've been studying English since ...

How long will you have been living in this place for when this year (or season) ends? I'll have been living in this place for ... when this year (or season) ends

Since when? Since ...

Notice that there is no important difference between saying "I have been living here for two months" and "I have lived here for two months". When speaking about duration, we can normally use either the perfect continuous tenses or the perfect tenses.

470 What's the difference between saying "I have been living here for two months" and "I have lived here for two months"? There is no important difference between saying ...

ruler

ultimo Gobernante

Who was the last ruler of your country?

The last ruler of my country was ...

Could you draw a completely straight line without the help of a ruler?

No, I couldn't ...

earth astronomical geographical

Generally speaking, what's the difference between "Earth" and "world"?

Generally speaking, ... is that we use the word "Earth" in the astronomical sense, and "world" in the geographical sense

How far's the Earth from the sun?

The Earth's about 93,000,000 miles from the sun (or 150,000,000 kilometres)

barro

What's mud?

Mud's a mixture of earth and water

by means of public transport

By what means can we draw a straight line?

We can draw ... by means of a pen or a pencil and a ruler

471 By what means do you come to school?

> mas bien

I come to school by (means of a) bus, train, car etc.

Would you rather have your own means of transport than use public transport?

Yes, I'd rather have ...
~ No, I wouldn't rather have ...

Why or why not?

As a means of making money, what would you say was the best way?

As a means ..., I'd say the best way was ...

figure

What's the best way to maintain a good figure?

The best way ...

Who do you think was the greatest figure in history?

I think ... was the greatest ...

How many figures are there in the number of your house?

There are ... figures in the number of my house

What kind of figure am I drawing in the air with my finger?

You're drawing a square
(a circle etc.) in the air with your finger

couple   adopt

If a couple can't have a child, what can they do?
If a couple …,
they can adopt one

If you went to live in another country, do you think you would quickly adopt the way of living in that country?
Yes, if I went to …,
I think I'd … ~ No, if I went to …, I don't think I'd …

Why or why not?

472 **cruel**

Who do you think was the cruellest character in history?
I think …
was the cruellest …

college

What's a college?
A college is a kind of school, or part of a university

burn

If we put a piece of wood or paper into a flame, what happens to it?
If we put …, it burns

take a bath

 Dictation 56

He won first prize/ for being the best student/ in his class./ I'm determined to carry on studying/ until I can speak English/ really well./ My dad taught me/ how to fix my bike./ He was a real gentleman,/ and showed good manners/ in all situations. / Although he is retired,/ he is still very famous/ and can't go out in public/ without being followed by a crowd./ Some people take mud baths/ for their health./ It was after midnight/ when the nurse got an opportunity/ to take a break./ What we eat influences/ the way we feel.

 *Do Revision Exercise 37*

LESSON 89

473 **run**

What are the three forms of "run"?

The three forms of
"run" are "run, ran, run"

What's the furthest you've ever run?

The furthest
I've ever run is ...

grow – grew – grown

What does the verb "to grow" mean?

The verb
"to grow" means "..."

What are the three forms of "grow"?

The three forms of
"grow" are "grow, grew, grown"

At about what age does the average person stop growing physically?

The average person ...

If you grew tired, what'd you do?

If I grew tired, I'd go to bed
and sleep, or sit down and rest

What kind of food is grown most of all in this part of the world?

The kind of food ... is ...

matter

What does the word "matter" mean?

The word
"matter" means "..."

What kind of matter is this book made of?

This book is
made of paper

474 Do you think that the possibility of another world war is a serious **matter**?

Yes, I think that ...

Are you interested in political matters?

Yes, I'm interested ...
~ No, I'm not interested ...

expect

How long do you expect to continue living in the place where you live now?

> I expect to continue ... where I live now for about ...

In a Callan Method lesson, do you expect the teacher to correct the students' mistakes?

> Yes, in a Callan Method lesson, I expect ...

Tail questions   tail   confirm

If somebody arrives home from work and they look very tired, instead of asking them "Are you feeling tired?", we could say "You're feeling tired, aren't you?" Here, we are using a tail question. We usually use a tail question when we believe something is true, and we want somebody to confirm that we are right.

When do we use a tail question?

> We use a tail question when we believe something is true, and we want somebody to confirm that we are right

With this kind of question, we first say what we believe is true (for example, "You're feeling tired") and then we put the tail question at the end (for example, "aren't you?"). We form the tail question by repeating the first auxiliary verb from the main part of the sentence, and putting it in question form.

How do we form a tail question?

> We form a tail question by repeating the first auxiliary verb from the main part of the sentence, and putting it in question form

Give me an example, please.

> He is going to go out tonight, isn't he?

475 **If the main part of the sentence is positive, the tail question is negative. If the main part of the sentence is negative, the tail question is positive.**

For example: **"You're Mr Brown, aren't you?"**

"You aren't Mr Brown, are you?"

Right, now I will say something and I want you to repeat it and add a tail question. Remember that, if the main part of the sentence is positive, the tail question is negative, and vice versa.

He's a young man.	He's a young man, isn't he?
He isn't a young man.	He isn't a young man, is he?
You've got a very nice kitchen..	You've got a very nice kitchen, haven't you?
You haven't got a very nice kitchen.	You haven't got a very nice kitchen, have you?
You can sing.	You can sing, can't you?
You can't sing.	You can't sing, can you?
He'll be afraid.	He'll be afraid, won't he?
He won't be afraid.	He won't be afraid, will he?
They would be hungry.	They would be hungry, wouldn't they?
They wouldn't be hungry.	They wouldn't be hungry, would they?

When there is no auxiliary verb in the main part of the sentence, we use the auxiliary verb "do" in the tail question. For example, "You know how to cook, don't you?"

476 When there is no auxiliary verb in the main part of the sentence, which verb do we use in the tail question ?

When there is no ..., we use "do" in the tail question

Give me an example, please.

They come every Thursday, don't they?

right	**legal**

If you had the right by law to do whatever you wished, what'd you do?

If I had the right by law to do whatever I wished, I'd ...

Do newspapers have the legal right to print stories that aren't true?

No, newspapers don't ...

Sobre
onto

We can use the word "on" for things that are moving or still. For example, we can say "I'm putting the book on the table" and also "The book is on the table". We can use the word "onto" only for things that are moving. We can say "I'm putting the book onto the table", but we can't say "The book is onto the table".

What's the difference between the words "on" and "onto"?

> The difference ... is that we can use the word "on" for things that are moving or still, whereas we can use the word "onto" only for things that are moving

Do you think you could jump onto the table with both your feet together?

> Yes, I think I could ...
> ~ No, I don't think I could ...

Have you ever tried to do something like that?

> Yes, I've tried to do something like that ~ No, I've never tried to do anything like that

477 **tie**

Do you know how to tie a tie?

> Yes, I know ...
> ~ No, I don't know ...

elect

In the past, was the government of a country generally elected by the people?

> No, in the past, the government ...

478 **to have something done**   **homework**

The structure "to have something done" communicates that we do not do the action ourselves, but that somebody else does it for us. For example, "I do not cut my hair myself; I have my hair cut by the hairdresser". Instead of saying "John is going to repair my computer for me", we can say "I am going to have my computer repaired by John".

What does the structure "to have something done" communicate?

> The structure "to have something done" communicates that we don't do the action ourselves, but that somebody else does it for us

Give me an example, please.

> I don't cut my hair myself; I have my hair cut by a hairdresser

Do you clean your shoes yourself or do you have them cleaned by someone else?

> I clean my shoes myself ~ I don't clean my shoes myself; I have them cleaned by someone else

Instead of the verb "to have" we can use the verb "to get". For example, "I got my hair cut yesterday".

What can we use instead of the verb "to have"?

> We can use the verb "to get" instead of ...

Do very young children sometimes get their homework done for them by their parents?

> Yes, very young children ...

power   **powerful**   **laptop**   **desktop**

Do you think governments generally have too much power?

> Yes, I think ... ~ No, I don't think ...

479 Who do you think is the most powerful person in this country?

> I think ... is the most ...

Do laptops use more power than desktop computers?

> No, laptops don't ...

save	rescue	protect	spend

The verb "save" can mean "to keep for the future", "to rescue", "to protect", and "to spend less".

Do you spend all your money or do you try to save some and put it in the bank?

> I spend all my money
> ~ I don't spend all my money;
> I try to save some and put it in the bank

If you saw someone in difficulty in the sea, how would you try to save their life?

> If I saw ..., I'd try to save their life by ...

What does an old man carry to save himself from falling over while walking?

> An old man carries a walking stick to save ...

Would you save any time if you used a different means of transport to come to school?

> Yes, I'd save some time if I ...
> ~ No, I wouldn't save any time if I ...

When you close a computer program, does it usually remind you to save your work first?

> Yes, when I ..., it usually reminds me to save my work first

Comercio   *artesano*   *cocion al horno*

trade	tradesman	skill	bake

panadero   *Carnicero*

baker	butcher	builder

What kind of things does your country mainly trade in?

> My country mainly trades in ...

480 **By a trade, we usually mean a job that a person does mainly with their hands, and for which they need a special skill. Some examples of tradesmen are bakers, butchers, builders etc.**

What do we usually mean by a trade?

> By a trade, we usually mean a ...

What's one of the best-paid trades in your country?

> One of the best-paid trades in my country is...

close /kləʊz/   close /kləʊs/

What's the difference between the words "close" /kləʊz/ and "close" /kləʊs/?   The difference between ... is that "close" /kləʊz/ is a verb meaning "shut", whereas "close" /kləʊs/ is an adjective meaning "near"

What's the closest you've ever been to real danger?   The closest I've ever been to real danger was when ...

trip   fortnight

A trip is a journey to a place and back again. For example, a business trip, a trip to the shops, a trip around the world etc.

If you went on a trip to New York, what would you see?   If I went ...., I'd see ...

When people go on business trips, do their companies usually pay for everything?   Yes, when people ...

Which would you prefer: an exciting trip to a big city for the weekend or a quiet fortnight on the beach?   I'd prefer ...

481   **every now and again**

de vez en cuando

What does the expression "every now and again" mean?   The expression "every now and again" means ...

Is it a good idea to give one's house a thorough cleaning from top to bottom every now and again?   Yes, it's a ...

no longer

What do you do with clothes that you no longer wear?   I ... clothes that I no longer wear

island

What's an island?   An island is a piece of land completely surrounded by water

ocean	Atlantic	Pacific	Indian

Name me some oceans, please.

The names ... are the Atlantic Ocean, the Pacific Ocean and the Indian Ocean

screen	DVD	CD

Do you prefer to watch films at home on DVD, or at the cinema on the big screen?

I prefer ...

Do you buy CDs and DVDs more often in the shops or online? I buy CDs ...

482 Is it bad for your eyes to look at a computer screen for too long?

Yes, it's bad ...

produce

What does your country produce?

My country produces ...

boast

What kind of things do people often boast about?

People often boast about their jobs, things that they own etc.

necessity

Is wearing a tie a necessity for some occupations these days?

Yes, wearing ...

 Dictation 57

To protect themselves from the rain,/ they threw themselves down/ under the big piece of wood/ that stood against the wall./ If they had not done so,/ they would have got/ thoroughly wet./ If we drive carelessly,/ we might have an accident./ However, driving too slowly/ is also fairly dangerous./ It is strange to think/ that from these small beginnings/ we will get a large tree./ I gave her some advice/ on caring for her dog./ Each member of a royal family/ has a title.

 *Do Revision Exercise 38*

483 **tell**   **say**

The most important difference between "tell" and "say" is that after "tell" we indicate the person we are speaking to, but after "say" we usually do not.

    For example: **I told David that I was going on holiday.**

                                   I said that I was going on holiday.

What's the most important difference between "tell" and "say"?

> The most important difference between "tell" and "say" is that after "tell" we indicate the person we are speaking to, but after "say" we usually do not

Give me an example, please.

> She told him that it was important.
> She said it was important.

After the verb "say", it is possible to indicate the person we are speaking to by using the word "to". For example: I said <u>to David</u> that I was going on holiday. After the verb "tell", however, we don't use "to".

After the verb "say", how is it possible to indicate the person we are speaking to?

> After the verb "say", it's possible to indicate the person we are speaking to by using the word "to"

With direct speech, we normally use the verb "say", and not "tell". For example: He said "I will see you tomorrow".

For direct speech, which verb do we normally use: "say" or "tell"?

> For direct speech, we normally use the verb "say"

Give me an example, please.

> She said "I'm hungry"

484 **With indirect speech, we can use either "say" or "tell", but we must use "tell" to report an order, not "say". For example: He told me to go downstairs.**

Which of these sentences is correct?

He told me to go away

or

He said me to go away

The first sentence – He told me to go away – is correct

risen

What are the three forms of "rise"?
The three forms of "rise" are "rise, rose, risen"

Have you ever risen before the sun has risen?
Yes, I've sometimes risen ... ~ No, I've never risen ...

gain   transaction   degree

The verb "to earn" generally means "to receive money for work done", whereas the verb "to gain" generally means "to get more of something". For example, we can gain strength, time, friends etc., or we can gain money through a business transaction.

What's the difference between "to earn" and "to gain"?
The difference between "to earn" and "to gain" is that the verb "to earn" ..., whereas the verb "to gain" ...

If you bought a business for £4 million and sold it later for half that amount, would you be gaining by doing so?
No, if I ..., I wouldn't be gaining by doing so; I'd be losing

How much would your loss be?
My loss would be £2 million

Does your watch generally gain or lose time, or does it keep perfect time?
My watch generally ...

485 What's the best way to gain friends?
The best way ... is to be nice to people

How long does it take the average student to gain a degree at university in your country?
It takes the average student about ... in my country

As regards learning a language, would you gain anything by going to the country where it was spoken?
Yes, as regards learning a language, I'd gain something by ...

Why?   Because I'd be able to speak the language every day

mark   **out of**   **petrol**

well-known   **trademark**

Are there any marks on these walls?   Yes, there are ...
                                                      ~ No, there aren't ...

What kind of marks are they?   They're ...

Who marks your dictations?   I mark my dictations myself

How many marks did you get in your last English exam?   I got ...
                                                      marks out of 100 in my ...

Which petrol company do you think has the most well-known trademark?
                          I think ... has the most well-known trademark

486   **base**   **basis**   **basic**

What part of the book is this?   It's the bottom,
                                                  or the base, of the book

What do you consider to be the basis of a good life?   I consider ... to be
                                                  the basis of a good life

Is it normal for language learners to continue making basic grammatical
mistakes even though they know the rules?   Yes, it's normal for ...

What do you think is basically the difference between your own language
and English?   I think that, basically,
                                the difference between my
                                own language and English is ...

include

When you stay at a hotel for one night, does the price you pay usually
include breakfast?   Yes, when you stay at ...
                                      ~ No, when you stay at ...

brush

What do we use to clean our shoes with?   We use a
                                                  shoe brush to clean ...

| What other kinds of brushes are there? | There are hairbrushes, toothbrushes, paintbrushes etc. |

box

| Do you like to watch boxing? | Yes, I like ... ~ No, I don't like ... |

Why or why not?

487 type

What type of film do you watch most?	I watch ...
Can you type?	Yes, I can type ~ No, I can't type
How many words a minute?	About ... words a minute

previous   occasion   wedding   video

| Have you met me on many previous occasions? | Yes, I've met you ... ~ No, I haven't met you ... |

Did you have any previous experience of the Callan Method before you came here?
Yes, I had some ... before I came here
~ No, I didn't have any ... before I came here

Why do people often make videos of special occasions like weddings?
People often ... so that they can remember them better

plan   interfere   interference

What do we mean by a street plan of a town?
By a ..., we mean a map showing the streets of the town and their names

Do you usually write your plans in a diary?
Yes, I usually write my ... ~ No, I don't usually write my ...

Do you think it's a good idea for teenagers to plan their futures whilst still at school?
Yes, I think ... ~ No, I don't think ...

Why or why not?

488 Do you think a young person should be allowed to plan their own future without the interference of their parents? Yes, I think ...
~ No, I don't think ...

Why or why not?

strange-looking

 *Dictation 58*

Some people/ have the manners of a pig./ Although he has lain in bed/ for several hours,/ he is still awake./ They did not notice/ the strange-looking house./ When people owe us a lot of money,/ we ought really to have a piece of paper/ with their signature on it/ and the amount they owe./ The servant took great pride/ in his work at the palace./ The lorry ran over some glass,/ and so we had to get out/ and change/ one of the wheels

LESSON 92

489 **The two types of auxiliary verb**

primary   **modal**

English has two basic types of auxiliary verb: primary auxiliaries and modal auxiliaries (or "modals").

What are the two basic types of auxiliary verb in English?
> The two basic types of auxiliary verb in English are primary auxiliaries and modal auxiliaries

There are three primary auxiliaries: "be", "have" and "do". We use them to make basic verb structures.

What are the primary auxiliaries?
> The primary auxiliaries are the verbs "be", "have" and "do"

We use the auxiliary "be" to make the continuous tenses, for example when we say "I am speaking English now". We also use it for the passive voice, for example when we say "This book was printed in England".

When do we use the auxiliary "be"?
> We use the auxiliary "be" to make the continuous tenses and the passive voice

Give me an example, please.
> I am speaking English now.
> This book was printed in England.

We use the auxiliary "have" for the perfect tenses, for example when we say "He has gone to Scotland".

When do we use the auxiliary "have"?
> We use the auxiliary "have" for the perfect tenses

490 Give me an example, please.
> He has gone to Scotland

We use the auxiliary "do" for the present simple and past simple, for example when we say "I don't speak Spanish" or "Did she eat the pasta?"

When do we use the auxiliary "do"?

We use the auxiliary "do" for the present simple and past simple

Give me an example, please.

I don't speak Spanish. Did she eat the pasta?

There are ten common modals: "can", "could", "will", "would", "may", "might", "shall", "should", "must" and "ought". Modals normally express ideas about necessity or possibility.

What are the ten common modals?

The ten common modals are "can", "could", "will", "would", "may", "might", "shall", "should", "must" and "ought"

What ideas do modals normally express?

Modals normally express ideas about necessity or possibility

Now, I will give you a sentence, and you say a sentence with the same meaning, but with a modal:

John is able to speak French.

John can speak French

Perhaps he works in a bank.

He may (or might) work in a bank

It is necessary for me to go to bed now.

I must go to bed now

You are not allowed to smoke in this building.

You can't (or mustn't) smoke in this building

After a modal, we put the infinitive without "to". For example, we say "I must go", and not "I must to go". The only exception to this rule is "ought". We say, for example, "I should call my mum soon", but if we express the same idea with "ought", we say "I ought <u>to</u> call my mum soon".

What do we put after a modal?

We put the infinitive without "to" after a modal

491 Give me an example, please.

I must send this email today

Which modal is the only exception to this rule?

"Ought" is the only exception to this rule

Give me an example, please.

I ought to see a doctor

set

What does the word "set" mean?

The word "set" means "..."

How long is the time set for a game of football? The time set ... is 90
minutes; that is, 45 minutes each way

What kind of life do you think is better: a life where you have a set time
for doing everything, such as eating, sleeping etc., or a life where you do
these things whenever you want? I think a life where you ... is
better than a life where you ...

What did I set down on the table when I came into the room at the
beginning of the lesson? You set your book
down on the table when you ...

If your watch isn't showing the right time, what do you have to do?
If my watch ..., I have to set it right

sunrise   **sunset**

What time is sunrise at the moment? Sunrise is at
about ... at the moment

And what time is sunset? Sunset is at about ...

492   **duty**   **society**   **on duty**

off duty   **driver**   **fine**

What do you consider to be the duty a person owes to the society in
which they live? I consider that the duty ...
is to be honest, hard-working etc.

What are the duties of a policeman? The duties ... are
to give people help and
information, catch criminals etc.

Do policemen wear their uniforms when they're off duty?
No, policemen don't wear ...; they
only wear them when they're on duty

If you brought a foreign car into this country, would you have to pay duty
on it? Yes, if I ..., I'd have to ... ~ No,
if I ..., I wouldn't have to ...

And if you didn't pay, what'd happen? If I didn't pay,
they might make me pay a fine,
and even take the car away from me

various

What are the various ways of learning a language?   The various ways ...
are at school with a teacher,
going to the country where the language is spoken,
practising with a friend, listening to the radio, watching TV etc.

entertainment

Is there much entertainment for teenagers in your home town?
Yes, there is a lot of ... in my home town
~ No, there isn't much ... in my home town

493   **weight**   **equal**

Is the weight of these two chairs about equal?   Yes, the weight of ...

operate   operation

Would you find it interesting to operate a factory machine?   Yes, I'd
find it ... ~ No, I wouldn't find it ...

Why or why not?

Have you ever had an operation in hospital?   Yes, I've had ... ~ No,
I've never had ...

 *Do Revision Exercise 39*

LESSON 93

494 **by**   **by the time**

When we are speaking about time, the word "by" can mean "at some point before" or "not later than". For example, "I will be home by midnight" means that I will arrive home at some point before midnight, or possibly at midnight, but certainly not later than midnight.

Give me a sentence containing the words "by the time".   By the time she
                                                    gets here, dinner will be ready

What does "by the time" mean in that sentence?   "By the time" in
                                              that sentence means at some point
                                              between now and when she gets here

By the time you are ninety years old, do you suppose your hair will be
grey?   Yes, by the time I'm ninety years old, I suppose my ...

Will your English have improved by this time next month?   Yes, my
                                                        English will ...

as well as

Can you speak English as well as you speak your own language?
                    No, I can't speak English as well as I speak my own
                    language; I speak it worse than my own language

Do you take English lessons on Sunday as well as during the week?
                                    Yes, I take ... ~ No, I don't take...

What does that last question mean in other words?   That last question
                              means "You take English lessons during
                   the week, but do you also take English lessons on Sunday?"

mayor

El mayor

495 **elder**   **eldest**

We generally use the words "elder" and "eldest" instead of "older" and "oldest" when speaking about people in the same family. However, we cannot say "elder than". For example, we cannot say "My sister is elder than me"; we must say "My sister is older than me".

What's the difference between the words "older" and "elder"?

The difference between ... is that we generally use the word "elder" when speaking about people in the same family, and we cannot say "elder than"

Have you got an elder brother?

Yes, I've got ... ~ No, I haven't got ...

Are you the eldest in your family?

Yes, I'm ... ~ No, I'm not ...

Who is?

Publicidad. *a cambio de.*

let   **rent**   **advertise**   **in exchange for**

The difference between "to let" and "to rent" is that "to let" means to lend something in exchange for money, whereas "to rent" means to borrow something in exchange for money.

↳ Pedir Prestado

What's the difference between "to let" and "to rent"?   The difference between "to let" and "to rent" ...

Supposing you had a house or a flat to let, how would you advertise it?

P Promedro

Supposing I had ..., I'd advertise it in the newspaper or on the internet

What's the average monthly rent for a small flat in this town?

The average ... is ...

496 How much does it cost to rent a car for one day in this town?   It costs about ...

Do you ever rent DVDs to watch at home?

Yes, I sometimes ... ~ No, I never ...

We can sometimes say "to rent out", instead of "to let".

Is it common in your country for people to rent out rooms in their house – to students, for example?

Yes, it's common in my country ... ~ No, it isn't common in my country ...

fallen

What are the three forms of "fall"?

The three forms of "fall" are "fall, fell, fallen"

Have you ever fallen out of bed in the middle of the night?

Yes, I've fallen ...

~ No, I've never fallen ...

chose

What's the past of the verb "to choose"?
The past of
the verb "to choose" is "chose"

Did you choose the clothes you're wearing yourself?
Yes, I chose the clothes I'm wearing
myself ~ No, I didn't choose the clothes I'm
wearing myself; someone else chose them for me

such a ...

Why do you suppose football is such a popular game?
I suppose
football is such a popular game because ...

497 Why is a desert such a difficult place to live in?
A desert is ... because
there is so little water

provide   providing   provided   ghost

Is a soldier's uniform provided for him by the government?
Yes, a
soldier's uniform is ...

How do parents provide for their children?
Parents ... by making
sure they have all the things they need in life

If you had just bought a house and then someone told you there was
a ghost in it, what would you do, providing, of course, you believed in
ghosts?
If I had just bought a house and
then someone told me there was a
ghost in it, I'd ..., providing I believed in ghosts

**In that last sentence, instead of using the word "providing", we could
have used "provided". Both forms have the same meaning.**

straight

Are you going to go straight home after the lesson?
Yes, I'm going
to go ... ~ No, I'm not going to go ...

If you came to some crossroads while driving a car and, instead of
stopping, you kept straight on, what might happen? If I came to ...
I kept straight on,
an accident might happen

consist

How many days does a fortnight consist of? A fortnight
consists of fourteen days

498 **place**

Why do we have to place an egg carefully on the table? We have to ...
because it could easily break

commence   academic

In which month does the academic year commence in your country?
The academic year ... in my country

colony

 *Dictation 59*

The plural of mouse is mice./ He got a bad throat/ from speaking too much./ The
colonies in America/ later developed/ into a large nation./ The TV was too loud,/ so
we turned it down./ They just could not understand/ the reason for their tiredness./
Some people like living alone;/ others hate it./ In my opinion,/ the kitchen is too
small./ There were several copies of the book/ in the library./ I cannot cycle any
further;/ I am too tired.

LESSON 94

499   **appear**   **disappear**   **appearance**

get to know

What's my hand doing?
> Your hand is appearing and disappearing (from under the table)

Does it appear to you that people in the world are becoming happier or less happy?
> It appears to me that ...

Why?

Do you judge people by appearances or do you wait until you get to know them well?
> I judge people by appearances ~ I don't judge people by appearances; I wait until I get to know them well

Which way of judging is fairer?
> Judging people after getting to know them well is fairer

double

If we double the number 25, what do we get?
> If we ..., we get 50

How wide is a double bed?
> A double bed is about double the width of a single bed

trouble   **take the trouble**   **look up**

dictionary   **modern**

500   Do you have trouble remembering all the rules of grammar in English?
> Yes, I have ... ~ No, I don't have ...

When children get into trouble, do they sometimes tell lies in order to get themselves out of trouble?
> Yes, when children ...

When you are reading a book in your own language and you see a word you don't know the meaning of, do you take the trouble to look it up in a dictionary or do you just keep on reading?
> When I'm reading ..., I take ... ~ When I'm reading ..., I don't take ...; I just ...

Do dreams sometimes trouble you at night?

> Yes, dreams sometimes trouble me at night
> ~ No, dreams never trouble me at night

What do you think is the trouble with modern life?

> I think the trouble ...

Change of spelling with comparison of adjectives

final   spelling

When an adjective ends in a single consonant preceded by a single vowel, the consonant is doubled when we form the comparative and superlative. For example, "big – bigger than – the biggest".

When do we double the final consonant of an adjective in forming its comparative and its superlative?

> We double the final ... when it ends in a single consonant preceded by a single vowel

Give me an example, please.

> thin – thinner than – the thinnest

When an adjective ends in a consonant plus "y", the "y" is changed to "i". For example, "happy – happier than – the happiest".

501 What happens when an adjective ends in a consonant plus "y"?

> When an adjective ..., the "y" is changed to "i"

Give me an example, please.

> lucky – luckier than – the luckiest

aungul

though

Give me an example of the word "though", please.

> I didn't like the food he cooked; I ate it though.
> Though she was feeling ill, she went on the business trip.

retagon

delay

When you have something unpleasant to do, do you delay doing it, or do you do it at once without delay?

> When I have ..., I delay doing it
> ~ When I have ..., I do it at once ...

Which is better though: to delay doing things or to do things at once without delay?

> It's usually better to do things at once without delay

When pupils are late for lessons, what kind of things have usually delayed them?   When pupils ..., the kind
of things that have ... are ...

across   come across   forest

What must you do before you walk across the road?   I must look both
ways before I ...

502 What can you see across the street (or road, field etc.) from this window?
I can see ... across
the street from this window

If you can't get across a river by bridge, how can you get across?
If you can't ..., you can get across
by boat or by swimming across

If you were walking in a forest and suddenly came across a tiger, what'd you do?   If I were ..., I'd ...

work   tell

If a lift isn't working, what do we have to do?   If a lift ...,
we have to take the stairs

Do you think it's possible to tell a person's character just by looking at their face?   Yes, I think ... ~ No, I don't think ...

Can we often tell where somebody comes from by their accent?   Yes,
we can ...

luggage   check in   check out

reception   receptionist

When you arrive at a hotel, where do you check in?   When you arrive
... at the reception desk

And what does the receptionist hand you when you've finished checking in?   The receptionist hands
you the key to the room when ...

On the day you leave a hotel, what time do you usually have to check out by?   On the day ... by noon

503 At the airport, do you usually check in all your luggage or do you carry some of it onto the plane with you?　At the airport, I usually check in all my luggage ~ At the airport, I usually carry some of my luggage onto the plane with me

defend

If someone says things about you which are not true, do you think it's better to defend yourself or just keep quiet?　If someone says things about me ..., I think ...

congratulations

On what occasions do we say "Congratulations!" to people?　We say ... when they pass an exam, get married, have a baby etc.

 *Dictation 60*

The arrow/ flew through the air/ and hit the tree/ in the middle./ He looked very strange;/ he had fair hair/ but a dark beard./ I do not know/ how much they gave him,/ but it was a large amount./ She goes to the same café/ every morning for a snack./ Poor John was not invited/ to Mary's birthday party./ I am sorry,/ but I have already thrown/ the old cooker away;/ it was too dangerous to keep.

 *Do Revision Exercise 40*

Grammar Questions

The following grammar questions are to be asked and revised in exactly the same way as any other questions in the Method. They act as a complete and rapid revision of all the grammar in Stages 5 and 6.

Stage 5

1) What's the difference between these two sentences: "I must study" and "I should study"?
The difference between those two sentences is that "I must study" means that I have no alternative, whereas "I should study" means I have alternatives but that studying is the right thing for me to do.

2) What can we use instead of "would be able" in conditional sentences? Give me an example.
We can use "could" instead of "would be able" in conditional sentences. For example, "If I was a bird, I could fly".

3) What's the difference between "still" and "yet"?
The difference between "still" and "yet" is that we use "still" for something that is in progress at the moment, whereas we use "yet" for something that has not begun or happened. We generally use "still" in positive sentences, whereas we generally use "yet" in questions and negative sentences.

4) What are the two ways of forming the 2nd conditional with the verb "to be"?
The two ways of forming the 2nd conditional with the verb "to be" are "if I was" and "if I were".

5) What's the difference between "for" and "since"? Give me some examples.
The difference between "for" and "since" is that we use the word "for" when we say a period of time, whereas we use the word "since" when we say the time at which a period began. For example, "for half an hour"; "for two weeks"; "since six o'clock"; "since last June".

6) When do we use the past continuous? Give me an example.
We use the past continuous for an action that was in progress at a particular time in the past. For example, "I was speaking English at this time yesterday".

7) What is the most common use of the past continuous? Give me an example. The most common use of the past continuous is to say that an action was in progress when another action happened. For example, "I was cooking lunch when she arrived".

8) What does the active voice communicate? The active voice communicates that the subject does the action.

9) What does the passive voice communicate? The passive voice communicates that the subject receives the action.

10) How do we form the passive voice? We form the passive voice with the verb "to be" and a past participle.

11) Change this sentence into the passive voice: "We are going to write the email". "The email is going to be written by us".

12) What are the two contracted forms of "you are not"? The two contracted forms of "you are not" are "you aren't" and "you're not".

13) What three things can the words "in spite of" and "despite" be followed by? Give me an example of each. "In spite of" and "despite" can be followed by a noun, or "-ing", or "the fact that ...". For example, "In spite of her illness, she went to work"; "Despite being ill, she went to work"; "In spite of the fact that she was ill, she went to work".

14) When do we use a reflexive pronoun? Give me an example. We use a reflexive pronoun when the subject and the object are the same person or thing. For example, "I looked at myself in the mirror".

15) What are the reflexive pronouns? The reflexive pronouns are "myself", "yourself", "himself", "herself", "itself", "oneself", "ourselves", "yourselves", and "themselves".

16) What is the most common way to communicate purpose in English? Give me an example. The most common way to communicate purpose in English is by using the infinitive with "to". For example, "I went to the hospital to see a doctor".

17) What's the difference between "to point at" and "to point out"?

The difference between "to point at" and "to point out" is that we use "to point at" for the action of pointing the finger at an object, whereas "to point out" means to indicate something among different things.

18) What do the words "may" and "might" express?

The words "may" and "might" express the idea of "perhaps".

19) What's the difference between "may" and "might"?

The difference between "may" and "might" is that we cannot use "may" in the 2nd conditional.

20) What does it mean when we add the word "back" to a verb? Give me some examples.

When we add the word "back" to a verb it means "to return". For example, "give back", "go back", "pay back" etc.

21) When do we use the past perfect? Give me an example.

We use the past perfect when we are thinking about time before and up to another point in the past. For example, "Mary could not enter her flat yesterday because she had lost her key".

22) Give me an example of the word "own" after a possessive adjective.

"This is my own book".

23) Where do the words "as well", "too" and "also" usually go?

The words "as well" and "too" go at the end of the sentence, but the word "also" usually goes after the first auxiliary verb.

24) Give me an example of "also" when there is no auxiliary verb.

I love coffee and I also love tea.

25) When do we use the future continuous? Give me an example.

We use the future continuous for an action that will be in progress at a particular time in the future. For example, "I will be working at this time tomorrow".

26) What's the difference between "allow" and "let"? Give me an example of each.

The difference between "allow" and "let" is that "allow" has the infinitive with "to" after it, whereas "let" has the infinitive without "to" after it. For example, "The doctor allowed me to change my appointment" and "The doctor let me change my appointment".

27) **What's the most common way to speak about our habits? Give me an example.**
The most common way to speak about our habits is to use the present simple or past simple. For example, "I play football every weekend"; "I always studied hard before exams at university".

28) **What's the difference between "travel" and "journey"?**
The difference between "travel" and "journey" is that we generally use "travel" as a verb and "journey" as a noun.

29) **What's the difference between the words "remember" and "remind"?**
The difference between the words "remember" and "remind" is that we remember something ourselves, without help, whereas, if we forget something, somebody reminds us. In other words, they remember for us.

30) **What's the difference between "to" and "at"? Give me an example of each.**
The difference between "to" and "at" is that we generally use "to" when we are moving in the direction of something, or somewhere, and "at" when we are there. For example, "I'm going to the table. Now, I'm at the table".

31) **When do we use the 3rd conditional? Give me an example.**
We use the 3rd conditional when we are imagining something in the past that did not really happen. For example, "If I had not come to school last week, I would have stayed at home".

32) **In the 3rd conditional, what do we put after the word "would"? Give me some examples.**
In the 3rd conditional, we put the word "have" and the past participle after the word "would". For example, "he would have slept"; "she would have written"; "they would have eaten".

33) **Give me an example of an adverb formed from an adjective.**
An example of an adverb formed from an adjective is "badly".

34) **How do we form the possessive case of a plural noun which already ends in "s"? Give me an example.**
We form the possessive case of a plural noun which already ends in "s" just by adding an apostrophe, but no "s". For example, "The girls' coats".

Stage 6

35) **When do we use the words "they", "them" etc. to talk about just one person? Give me an example.** We use the words "they", "them" etc. to talk about just one person when we don't know if the person is a man or woman. For example, "There is somebody at the door. Go and see what they want".

36) **What's the grammatical difference between "would rather" and "would prefer"? Give me an example of each.** The grammatical difference between "would rather" and "would prefer" is that we put the infinitive without "to" after "would rather", whereas we put the infinitive with "to" after "would prefer". For example, "I would rather drink tea" and "I would prefer to drink tea".

37) **What are two common uses of the future simple? Give me an example of each.** Two common uses of the future simple are to communicate that we have just this moment decided to do something, and to make a prediction. For example, "Sorry I forgot to bring the money for you; I'll bring it tomorrow, I promise!" and "I can't remember what she looks like but I'm sure I'll recognize her when I see her".

38) **What are two common uses of "to be going to"? Give me an example of each, please.** Two common uses of "to be going to" are to make a prediction using information we already have, and to communicate a future intention. For example, "Be careful; that wine glass is going to fall off the table!" and "I'm going to go to the cinema next Saturday".

39) **When do we use the auxiliary verb "do" in a positive sentence with the present simple tense?** We use the auxiliary verb "do" in a positive sentence with the present simple tense when we want to be emphatic.

40) **When do we usually use the emphatic "do"? Give me an example.** We usually use the emphatic "do" when we want to deny something that someone has said because we know it is not true. For example, if somebody says "You don't eat enough vegetables", I can reply "Yes I do eat enough vegetables!"

41) **What is another use of the emphatic "do"? Give me an example.**

Another use of the emphatic "do" is in an exclamation. For example, "I do hate noisy children".

42) **How do we form the future perfect?**

We form the future perfect with the verb "to have" and a past participle.

43) **When do we use the future perfect? Give me an example.**

We use the future perfect when we are thinking about time before and up to a point in the future. For example, "When you arrive at my house, I'll have cooked dinner".

44) **Give me an example of direct speech.**

Mr Brown said "I like warm weather".

45) **Give me an example of indirect speech.**

Mr Brown said that he liked warm weather.

46) **What do we do with the tenses when we change direct speech into indirect speech? Give me an example.**

When we change direct speech into indirect speech, we generally move the verb into the past. For example: The teacher said "The room is large". The teacher said that the room was large.

47) **What do we do if a verb is already in the past?**

If a verb is already in the past, it often remains unchanged, but sometimes we put it further into the past.

48) **What do we do with the word "will" when we change direct speech into indirect speech? Give me an example.**

When we change direct speech into indirect speech, we change the word "will" to "would". For example: She said that John would go to London next year.

49) **What's the difference between the words "what" and "whatever"? Give me an example of "whatever".**

The difference between the words "what" and "whatever" is that we use the word "what" in a limited sense, whereas we use the word "whatever" in a more unlimited sense. For example, "If I could buy whatever I wanted, I'd buy ...".

50) **Tell me four common ways in which we can make a suggestion.**

Four common ways in which we can make a suggestion are:
Shall we wait for him?
Let's wait for him.
How (or What) about waiting for him?
Why don't we wait for him?

51) How do we make the imperative in English? Give me some examples.

We make the imperative in English by using the infinitive without "to". For example, "Give me the book!"; "Do it now!"; "Have a nice day!"

52) How do we make a negative imperative? Give me some examples.

We make a negative imperative by putting the word "don't" before the infinitive. For example, "Don't give him the book!"; "Don't be late!"; "Don't forget to email me!"

53) How do we form the perfect continuous tenses? Give me an example.

We form the perfect continuous tenses by using the verb "have", the word "been", and the present participle of the main verb. For example, "I have been studying for two hours".

54) When do we use the present perfect continuous? Give me an example.

We use the present perfect continuous to say how long an action has been in progress so far. For example, "I have been living in this house for six months so far".

55) When do we use the past perfect continuous? Give me an example.

We use the past perfect continuous to communicate the duration of an action up to a particular point in the past. For example, "I had been living in this house for one month when I bought my new bed".

56) When do we use the future perfect continuous? Give me an example.

We use the future perfect continuous to communicate the duration of an action up to a particular point in the future. For example, "I will have been living in this house for eight months at the end of this year".

57) When do we use a tail question?

We use a tail question when we believe something is true, and we want somebody to confirm that we are right.

58) How do we form a tail question? Give me an example.

We form a tail question by repeating the first auxiliary verb from the main part of the sentence, and putting it in question form. For example, "He is going to go out tonight, isn't he?"

59) When there is no auxiliary verb in the main part of the sentence, which verb do we use in the tail question? Give me an example.

When there is no auxiliary verb in the main part of the sentence, we use "do" in the tail question. For example, "They come every Thursday, don't they?"

60) What does the structure "to have something done" communicate? Give me an example.

The structure "to have something done" communicates that we don't do the action ourselves, but that somebody else does it for us. For example, "I don't cut my hair myself; I have my hair cut by a hairdresser".

61) What's the most important difference between "tell" and "say"? Give me an example.

The most important difference between "tell" and "say" is that after "tell" we indicate the person we are speaking to, but after "say" we usually do not. For example: She told him that it was important. She said it was important.

62) After the verb "say", how is it possible to indicate the person we are speaking to?

After the verb "say", it is possible to indicate the person we are speaking to by using the word "to".

63) For direct speech, which verb do we normally use: "say" or "tell"? Give me an example.

For direct speech, we normally use the verb "say". For example: She said "I'm hungry".

64) What are the two basic types of auxiliary verb in English?

The two basic types of auxiliary verb in English are primary auxiliaries and modal auxiliaries.

65) What are the primary auxiliaries?

The primary auxiliaries are the verbs "be", "have" and "do".

66) When do we use the auxiliary "be"? Give me an example.

We use the auxiliary "be" to make the continuous tenses and the passive voice. For example, "I am speaking English now" and "This book was printed in England".

67) When do we use the auxiliary "have"? Give me an example.

We use the auxiliary "have" for the perfect tenses. For example, "He has gone to Scotland".

68) When do we use the auxiliary "do"? Give me an example.

We use the auxiliary "do" for the present simple and past simple. For example, "I don't speak Spanish" and "Did she eat the pasta?"

69) What are the ten common modals?

The ten common modals are "can", "could", "will", "would", "may", "might", "shall", should", "must" and "ought".

70) What do we put after a modal? Give me an example.

We put the infinitive without "to" after a modal. For example, "I must send this email today".

71) Which modal is the only exception to this rule? Give me an example.

"Ought" is the only exception to this rule. For example, "I ought to see a doctor".

72) Give me a sentence containing the words "by the time".

For example, "By the time she gets here, dinner will be ready".

73) What does "by the time" mean in that sentence?

"By the time" in that sentence means at some point between now and when she gets here.

74) What's the difference between the words "older" and "elder"?

The difference between the words "older" and "elder" is that we generally use the word "elder" when speaking about people in the same family, and we cannot say "elder than"

75) When do we double the final consonant of an adjective in forming its comparative and its superlative? Give me an example.

We double the final consonant of an adjective in forming its comparative and its superlative when it ends in a single consonant preceded by a single vowel. For example, "thin – thinner than – the thinnest".

76) What happens when an adjective ends in a consonant plus "y"? Give me an example.

When an adjective ends in a consonant plus "y", the "y" is changed to "i". For example, "lucky – luckier than – the luckiest".

List of tenses and other verb forms

The following is a list of all the tenses and other verb forms used in Stages 5 and 6. The students should read them through as part of the last lesson.

Past continuous

I was working – I was not working – Was I working?

Past perfect

I had worked – I had not worked – Had I worked?

Future continuous

I will be working – I will not be working – Will I be working?

3rd conditional

If I had worked …, I would have …

Future perfect

I will have worked – I will not have worked – Will I have worked?

Imperative

Work! – Don't work!

Past perfect continuous

I had been working – I had not been working – Had I been working?

Present perfect continuous

I have been working – I have not been working – Have I been working?

Future perfect continuous

I will have been working – I will not have been working – Will I have been working?

Revision Exercise 32 (Lessons 68 – 69)

1 Name some foods that are very popular despite being bad for the health.

2 Do you think it's worth learning a foreign language in spite of the fact that it's quite difficult?

3 When your shoes look dirty, what do you do?

4 In your country, do you have to buy a ticket before getting on a bus?

5 How do we get mud on our shoes?

6 Are the buses in this town usually crowded in the morning?

7 Which is the widest street in the place where you live, and which is the narrowest?

8 Do you know the origin of your national flag?

9 If you got wet, what'd you have to do with your clothes?

10 Did you wash yourself when you were a baby?

11 What kind of things make you thoroughly tired?

12 If you took something by accident that didn't belong to you, what'd you do?

13 Do people become careless when they're in great danger?

14 Who owns the place where you live?

15 Do people in your country usually carry on working after the age of sixty-five?

16 Is English the most widely spoken language in the world?

17 Do people in very hot countries dress in the same manner as people in very cold countries?

18 Who takes care of us when we're in hospital?

19 For what purpose do people work?

20 What's the difference between "to point at" and "to point out"?

Answers

1 Some foods that are very popular despite being bad for the health are ...

2 Yes, I think it's worth learning a foreign language in spite of the fact that it's quite difficult.

3 When my shoes look dirty, I clean them.

4   Yes, in my country, you have to buy a ticket before getting on a bus. ~ No, in my country, you don't have to buy a ticket before getting on a bus; you can just pay when you get on.

5   We get mud on our shoes by walking in the countryside in the rain.

6   Yes, the buses in this town are usually crowded in the morning. ~ No, the buses in this aren't town usually crowded in the morning.

7   ... is the widest street in the place where I live, and ...is the narrowest.

8   Yes, I know the origin of my national flag. ~ No, I don't know the origin of my national flag.

9   If I got wet, I'd have to take my clothes off and hang them up to dry.

10   No, I didn't wash myself when I was a baby; my mother washed me.

11   The kind of things that make me thoroughly tired are hard physical work, studying a lot without a break, not enough sleep etc.

12   If I took something by accident that didn't belong to me, I'd return it.

13   No, people don't become careless when they're in great danger; they become very careful.

14   ... own(s) the place where I live. ~ I don't know who owns the place where I live.

15   Yes, people in my country usually carry on working after the age of sixty-five. ~ No, people in my country don't usually carry on working after the age of sixty-five; they retire.

16   Yes, English is the most widely spoken language in the world.

17   No, people in very hot countries don't dress in the same manner as people in very cold countries; they dress in a different manner.

18   Nurses and doctors take care of us when we're in hospital.

19   People work in order to earn money.

20   The difference between "to point at" and "to point out" is that we use "to point at" for the action of pointing the finger at an object, whereas" to point out" means to indicate something among different things.

1   What might happen if you didn't look both ways before crossing the road?

2   What's the difference between "arrive at" and "arrive in"?

3   What is a café?

4   When you go on holiday, what do you bring back with you?

5   Do people normally feel proud when they do well in exams?

6   If you were very rich, would you have servants in your house?

7   Does a lorry have fewer wheels than a car?

8   Do you know anybody who has a long beard?

9   Is everything we read in the newspapers true?

10 Which is further from Spain: Sweden or Switzerland?

11 When do we use the past perfect?

12 When you began your lessons at this school, had you already studied some English or were you a complete beginner?

13 Which is the strongest political party in your country today?

14 What kind of things are you most mad about?

15 If you were given two copies of the same book for your birthday, what would you do?

16 What do mice like eating?

17 Where do we find sand?

18 What do you do when you arrive at somebody's front door in order to pay a visit?

19 Which animals like to fetch sticks that you throw for them?

20 This evening, would you prefer to go out for dinner or simply go home?

Answers

1   An accident might happen if I didn't look both ways before crossing the road.

2   The difference between "arrive at" and "arrive in" is that we arrive at a point, whereas we arrive in an area.

3   A café is a small, informal restaurant where you can get light meals, snacks and drinks.

4   When I go on holiday, I bring back souvenirs with me.

5   Yes, people normally feel proud when they do well in exams.

6   Yes, if I were very rich, I'd have servants in my house. ~ No, if I were very rich, I wouldn't have servants in my house.

7   No, a lorry doesn't have fewer wheels than a car; it has more wheels.

8   Yes, I know somebody who has a long beard. ~ No I don't know anybody who has a long beard.

9   No, not everything we read in the newspapers is true; some things are true and some things are false.

10   Sweden is further from Spain than Switzerland.

11   We use the past perfect when we are thinking about time before and up to another point in the past.

12   When I began my lessons at this school, I had already studied some English. ~ When I began my lessons at this school, I hadn't studied any English; I was a complete beginner.

13   The ... party is the strongest political party in my country today.

14   I'm most mad about music, films, sport etc.

15   If I were given two copies of the same book for my birthday, I'd ...

16   Mice like eating cheese etc.

17   We find sand on a beach, in a desert etc.

18   When I arrive at somebody's front door in order to pay a visit, I knock on the door or ring the door-bell.

19   Dogs like to fetch sticks that you throw for them.

20   This evening, I'd prefer to ...

Revision Exercise 34 (Lessons 72 – 73)

1   Are you already able to speak English without making any mistakes?

2   What's the reason for tiredness?

3   Do you live alone or with other people?

4   What would you say was the best way to remember something?

5   Should we always give back the things we borrow?

6 Do you live in your own house (flat), or does it belong to somebody else?

7 What do we mean by a wireless internet connection?

8 Tell me three ways of cooking potatoes.

9 What's a wall normally built of?

10 Give me an example of "also" when there is no auxiliary verb, please.

11 When do we use the future continuous?

12 Where do you think you'll be living in ten years' time?

13 Is a yard longer than a metre?

14 What do we mean when we say someone is a chain-smoker?

15 Are you wearing a belt?

16 Is the cost of living constantly rising these days?

17 Do most radio stations have hourly traffic news?

18 What's the difference between "allow" and "let"?

19 What sometimes happens when we let people borrow things that belong to us?

20 Do you think students should be allowed to use their mobile phones during lessons?

Answers

1 No, I'm not able to speak English without making any mistakes yet; I still make some mistakes.

2 The reason for tiredness is too much work, not enough sleep etc.

3 I live alone. ~ I live with other people.

4 I'd say that the best way to remember something was to repeat it often.

5 Yes, we should always give back the things we borrow.

6 Yes, I live in my own house (flat). ~ No, I don't live in my own house (flat); it belongs to ...

7 By a wireless internet connection, we mean that we can connect to the internet without connecting wires to our computer.

8 Three ways of cooking potatoes are boiling, frying and roasting.

9 A wall is normally built of bricks.

10 I love coffee and I also love tea.

11 We use the future continuous for an action that will be in progress at a particular time in the future.

12 I think I'll be living ... in ten years' time.

13 No, a yard isn't longer than a metre; it's a little shorter than a metre.

14 When we say someone is a chain-smoker, we mean that he smokes one cigarette after another without stopping, like a chain.

15 Yes, I'm wearing a belt. ~ No, I'm not wearing a belt.

16 Yes, the cost of living is constantly rising these days. ~ No, the cost of living isn't constantly rising these days.

17 Yes, most radio stations have hourly traffic news.

18 The difference between "allow" and "let" is that "allow" has the infinitive with "to" after it, whereas "let" has the infinitive without "to" after it.

19 When we let people borrow things that belong to us, they sometimes don't return them.

20 Yes, I think students should be allowed to use their mobile phones during lessons. ~ No, I don't think students should be allowed to use their mobile phones during lessons.

Revision Exercise 35 (Lessons 74 – 75)

1 Is there anywhere near here I can buy foreign books?

2 Where in the world can a man murder another man without breaking the law?

3 Why does a man sometimes loosen his tie?

4 What do we sometimes see and hear in a storm?

5 How do blind people read?

6 Where does the devil live?

7 What's another way of saying "I ride a bike every day"?

8 What words do we use when we ask permission to do something?

9 If you walked in the rain without carrying an umbrella or wearing a raincoat, what might happen?

10 Are you in the habit of speaking to yourself when you're alone?

11 What's the difference between a stranger and a foreigner?

12 Do you think it looks like rain (or looks as if it is going to rain)?

13 What's the difference between "travel" and "journey"?

14 Have you suffered from any illnesses in the last two years?

15 What's your greatest wish in life?

16 What's the difference between the words "remember" and "remind"?

17 What's the difference between a bookshop and a library?

18 Are there some areas of the world where it never gets warm, even in the middle of summer?

19 Are you coming to the school?

20 Which would get you home sooner: a bus or a car?

Answers

1 Yes, there's somewhere near here you can buy foreign books

2 There's nowhere in the world where a man can murder another man without breaking the law.

3 A man sometimes loosens his tie because it's more comfortable.

4 We sometimes see lightning and hear thunder in a storm.

5 Blind people read with special books made for them, which they can read by touching the words.

6 The devil lives in hell.

7 Another way of saying "I ride a bike every day" is "I cycle every day".

8 We use "may", "can" or "could" when we ask permission to do something.

9 If I walked in the rain without carrying an umbrella or wearing a raincoat, I'd get wet and might catch a cold.

10 Yes, I'm in the habit of speaking to myself when I'm alone. ~ No, I'm not in the habit of speaking to myself when I'm alone.

11 The difference between a stranger and a foreigner is that a stranger is somebody we don't know whereas a foreigner is somebody from another country.

12 Yes, I think it looks like rain. ~ No, I don't think it looks like rain.

13 The difference between travel and journey is that we generally use travel as a verb and journey as a noun.

14 Yes, I've suffered from some illnesses in the last two years. ~ No, I haven't suffered from any illnesses in the last two years.

15 My greatest wish in life is ...

16 The difference between remember and remind is that we remember something ourselves, without help, whereas, if we forget something, somebody reminds us.

17 The difference between a bookshop and a library is that a bookshop is a place where we can buy books, whereas a library is a place where we can go to read books and borrow them.

18 Yes, there are some areas of the world where it never gets warm, even in the middle of summer.

19 No, I'm not coming to the school; I'm at the school.

20 I think maybe a car would get me home sooner than a bus.

Revision Exercise 36 (Lessons 76 – 77)

1   What would you do if you needed a haircut?

2   What does the word "towards" mean?

3   Where is the nearest sports stadium?

4   Why is a Rolls Royce much more expensive than an ordinary car?

5   If your body temperature falls a lot, what should you do?

6   If you have a problem with your teeth, who should you go to see?

7   Does it seem warmer to you today than it was yesterday?

8   How many letters is the English alphabet composed of?

9   Do you think wisdom comes more with age or experience?

10 What's the greatest physical pain you've ever suffered?

11 When a car park is full, where does a driver have to park his car?

12 When do we use the 3rd conditional?

13 What is its construction?

14 If you had been born in England, which language would you have spoken as a child?

15 What kind of character do you like to see in a person?

16   If you were driving a car on a long journey and suddenly felt really tired, what would you do?

17   Why do even the best tennis players need a coach?

18   Tell me one very common way of forming adverbs from adjectives and give me an example, please.

19   What do footballers' shirts have written on their backs?

20   Can the English coast be seen from the coast of France?

Answers

1   If I needed a haircut, I'd go to a hairdresser's.

2   The word "towards" means "in the direction of".

3   The nearest sports stadium is ...

4   A Rolls Royce is much more expensive than an ordinary car because it takes longer to make than an ordinary car.

5   If my body temperature falls a lot, I should go to bed and call a doctor.

6   If I have a problem with my teeth, I should go to see a dentist.

7   Yes, it seems warmer to me today than it was yesterday. ~ No, it doesn't seem warmer to me today than it was yesterday; it seems cooler.

8   The English alphabet is composed of 26 letters.

9   I think wisdom comes more with ... than ...

10   The greatest physical pain I've ever suffered was ...

11   When a car park is full, a driver has to park his car in the street.

12   We use the 3rd conditional when we are imagining something in the past that did not really happen.

13   Its construction is "If" + past perfect + "would have done".

14   If I had been born in England, I would have spoken English as a child.

15   I like to see a ... character in a person.

16   If I were driving a car on a long journey and suddenly felt really tired, I'd stop the car, buy a cup of coffee, and wait until I felt more awake.

17   Even the best tennis players need a coach to help them to improve their game.

18   One very common way of forming adverbs from adjectives is by adding the letters "ly" to the adjective; e.g. bad-badly.

19   Footballers' shirts have numbers written on their backs.

20   Yes, on certain days, the English coast can be seen from the coast of France.

Revision Exercise 37 (Lessons 78 – 79)

1   Do police officers often find themselves in dangerous situations?

2   What do you suppose'd happen if there were suddenly no water in the world?

3   Does good wine usually become cheaper and cheaper as it becomes older?

4   How long does it take you to get ready to go out in the morning?

5   Describe the place where you live.

6   Is it correct to say "the book was writing by him"?

7   What'll you do as soon as the lesson is over?

8   If someone lost their passport, what advice would you give them?

9   If some friends were talking loudly while you were trying to study, what would you say?

10   Do you always choose your clothes yourself or does someone else ever help you to choose them?

11   What can we say instead of "I would prefer to drink tea"?

12   Which would you rather do this evening: read a book, watch television, or go to the cinema?

13   Do you have very much faith in your government?

14   Tell me what you have decided to do this evening, please.

15   Are most people busy on Sunday?

16   Would you say you were good at recognizing people after not having seen them for several years?

17   If you had to get to a room that was on the tenth floor of a building, would you take the stairs or the lift?

18   Do you think women look better with or without lipstick?

19   What system of government do you have in your country?

20   Is sailing a popular sport in your country?

Answers

1 Yes, police officers often find themselves in dangerous situations.

2 I suppose we'd all die of thirst if there were suddenly no water in the world.

3 No, good wine doesn't usually become cheaper and cheaper as it becomes older; it usually becomes more and more expensive.

4 It takes me about ... to get ready to go out in the morning.

5 The place where I live is (by the sea; it's quite large; there are some factories just outside it etc.).

6 No, it isn't correct to say "the book was writing by him"; we must say "The book was written by him".

7 I'll stand up, go home etc. as soon as the lesson is over.

8 If someone lost their passport, I'd tell them that they should immediately go to the police.

9 If some friends were talking loudly while I was trying to study, I'd say "Could you be quiet, please?"

10 Yes, I always choose my clothes myself. ~ No, I don't always choose clothes myself; sometimes someone helps me to choose them.

11 We can say "I would rather drink tea" instead of "I would prefer to drink tea".

12 I'd rather ... than ...

13 Yes, I have a lot of faith in my government. ~ No, I don't have very much faith in my government.

14 This evening, I'm going to visit a friend etc.

15 No, most people aren't busy on Sunday; they're free.

16 Yes, I'd say I was good at recognizing people after not having seen them for several years. ~ No, I wouldn't say I was good at recognizing people after not having seen them for several years.

17 If I had to get to a room that was on the tenth floor of a building, I'd take the lift.

18 I think women look better ... lipstick.

19 We have a ... system of government in my country.

20 Yes, sailing's a popular sport in my country. ~ No, sailing isn't a popular sport in my country.

Revision Exercise 38 (Lessons 80 – 81)

1 When do we use the auxiliary verb "do" in a positive sentence with the present simple tense?

2 When do we usually use the emphatic "do"?

3 Reply to this sentence using an emphatic form in the past, please: He didn't cycle home yesterday.

4 Reply to this sentence using the emphatic form, please: The weather's been good.

5 What'd happen if you hit a policeman?

6 What are the five meanings of the word "fair"?

7 Do people become darker and darker in hair colour as we go towards the north of Europe?

8 Do you speak English fairly well now?

9 Is it a great pleasure for you to get up in the morning?

10 Are you against animals being used for experiments?

11 When was America discovered by Europeans, and who discovered it?

12 Would you like to be a scientist?

13 Do you think life will be discovered on other planets within the next hundred years?

14 Do you think that the difference between the people of one country and those of another is mainly a question of language?

15 Why are people so often in the habit of singing to themselves in the bathroom?

16 If you bought a business for £1,000,000 and sold it again later for £250,000, would you be making a profit?

17 When do we use the future perfect? Give me an example, please

18 What's the difference between these two sentences? "At 9 o'clock, I will eat my dinner" and "At 9 o'clock, I will have eaten my dinner"

19 What do some countries call the most important minister in the government?

20 Are you usually able to guess a person's age?

Answers

1. We use the auxiliary verb "do" in a positive sentence with the present simple tense when we want to be emphatic.

2. We usually use the emphatic "do" when we want to deny something that someone has said because we know it is not true.

3. Yes he did cycle home yesterday!

4. No the weather has not been good!

5. If I hit a policeman, he'd arrest me.

6. The five meanings of the word "fair" are: the opposite of dark (e.g. hair), industrial/agricultural fair, just, moderate and funfair.

7. No, people don't become darker and darker in hair colour as we go towards the north of Europe; they become fairer and fairer.

8. Yes, I speak English fairly well now.

9. Yes, it's a great pleasure for me to get up in the morning. ~ No, it isn't a great pleasure for me to get up in the morning.

10. Yes, I'm against animals being used for experiments. ~ No, I'm not against animals being used for experiments.

11. America was discovered by Europeans in 1492 by Christopher Columbus, or by Leif Ericsson about the year 1000.

12. Yes, I'd like to be a scientist. ~ No, I wouldn't like to be a scientist.

13. Yes, I think life will be discovered on other planets within the next hundred years. ~ No, I don't think life will be discovered on other planets within the next hundred years.

14. Yes, I think that the difference between the people of one country and those of another is mainly a question of language. ~ No, I don't think that the difference between the people of one country and those of another is mainly a question of language.

15. People are so often in the habit of singing to themselves in the bathroom maybe because their voices sound better in the bathroom.

16. No, if I bought a business for £1,000,000 and sold it again later for £250,000, I wouldn't be making a profit; I'd be making a loss.

17. We use the future perfect when we are thinking about time before and up to a specific point in the future. When you arrive at my house, I will have cooked dinner.

18 The difference between these (those) two sentences is that "At 9 o'clock, I will eat my dinner" means I will start to eat my dinner at 9 o'clock, whereas "At 9 o'clock, I will have eaten my dinner" means that my dinner will already be finished at 9 o'clock.

19 Some countries call the most important minister in the government the Prime Minister.

20 Yes, I'm usually able to guess a person's age. ~ No, I'm not usually able to guess a person's age.

Revision Exercise 39 (Lessons 82 – 83)

1   If you rode from here to the next town by bicycle, about how long would it take you?

2   Do you have to join a library before you can start borrowing books?

3   When you fill in a passport application form, what must you state?

4   When you make a formal written statement to the police, do you have to put your signature at the end?

5   What kind of things can we download from the internet?

6   What happens if someone drinks too much alcohol?

7   What's the difference between "mind" and "brain"?

8   What happens to criminals if the police catch them?

9   Do you think the world's more civilized nowadays than it was in the past?

10 What does the expression "so far, so good" mean?

11 Answer the following question with a short answer: did people believe the world was round in the old days?

12 Did the sun rise early this morning?

13 About how many kilometres are there in a mile?

14 If you fell over while you were running along the street, might you hurt yourself?

15 Would you be glad if you were told you had won the lottery?

16 What's another meaning of "to be sick" besides "to be unwell"?

17 When things break, do you normally try to repair them or do you just throw them away?

18   What do we call the top covering of a house?

19   Is it a windy day today?

20   When was the last time you caught a cold?

Answers

1   If I rode from here to the next town by bicycle, it'd take me about ...

2   Yes, you have to join a library before you can start borrowing books.

3   When I fill in a passport application form, I must state my name, my address, my date of birth, my occupation etc.

4   Yes, when you make a formal written statement to the police, you have to put your signature at the end.

5   We can download programs, songs, films etc. from the internet.

6   If someone drinks too much alcohol, they get drunk.

7   The difference between "mind" and "brain" is that we use "mind" in the abstract sense, whereas we generally use "brain" in the physical sense.

8   If the police catch criminals, they arrest them and take them to the police station.

9   Yes, I think the world's more civilized nowadays than it was in the past. ~ No, I don't think the world's more civilized nowadays than it was in the past; I think it's less civilized.

10   The expression "so far, so good" means that somebody has not experienced any problems up to now.

11   No, they didn't.

12   Yes, the sun rose early this morning. ~ No, the sun didn't rise early this morning; it rose late.

13   There are about 1.6 kilometres in a mile.

14   Yes, if I fell over while I was running along the street, I might hurt myself.

15   Yes, I'd be glad if I were told I'd won the lottery.

16   Another meaning of "to be sick" besides "to be unwell" is "to vomit".

17   When things break, I normally try to repair them/just throw them away

18   We call the top covering of a house the roof.

19   Yes, it's a windy day today. ~ No, it isn't a windy day today.

20   The last time I caught a cold was ...

Revision Exercise 40 (Lessons 84 – 85)

1   What are the two ways in which we can repeat what someone has said?

2   What do we call these two ways?

3   Give me an example of direct speech, please.

4   Give me an example of indirect speech, please.

5   What do we do with the tenses when we change direct speech into indirect speech?

6   What do we do if a verb is already in the past?

7   What do we do with the word "will" when we change direct speech into indirect speech?

8   "I swim every day" – what did I say? (use indirect speech)

9   "I ate too much for dinner" – what did I say?

10 Did people in the old days believe the world was round?

11 What kind of people do you pity most?

12 Have you ever been blown off your feet by the wind?

13 Why must we consider carefully before making an important decision?

14 If you could go wherever you liked in the world, where'd you go?

15 Do newspapers always tell the truth?

16 How long do you have to be away from home before you begin to miss your family and friends?

17 What is a trade union?

18 Where do people go when they are looking for justice?

19 How do we form verbs from certain adjectives or nouns?

20 If our trousers are too long, what must we do to them?

Answers

1   The two ways in which we can repeat what someone has said are by giving the exact words of the speaker, or by reporting what the speaker said.

2   We call these two ways direct speech and indirect speech.

3   Mr. Brown said "I like warm weather".

4 Mr. Brown said that he liked warm weather.

5 When we change direct speech into indirect speech, we generally move the verb into the past.

6 If a verb is already in the past, it often remains unchanged, but sometimes we put it further into the past.

7 When we change direct speech into indirect speech, we change the word "will" to "would".

8 You said that you swam every day.

9 You said you had eaten too much for dinner.

10 No, people in the old days didn't believe the world was round; they believed it was flat.

11 I pity ... most.

12 Yes, I've been blown off my feet by the wind. ~ No, I've never been blown off my feet by the wind.

13 We must consider carefully before making an important decision because, if we don't consider carefully, we might make a big mistake.

14 If I could go wherever I liked in the world, I'd go to ...

15 No, newspapers don't always tell the truth; sometimes they tell lies.

16 I have to be away from home for about ... before I begin to miss my family and friends.

17 A Trade Union is an organization composed of workers from a particular industry. It protects the workers and fights to improve their pay and conditions.

18 People go to the law courts when they are looking for justice.

19 We form verbs from certain adjectives or nouns by adding the letters "en".

20 If our trousers are too long, we must shorten them.

Index

Notes

Notes